That's My Crowd!

by

Dr. Shelton Smith

Post Office Box 1099 • Murfreesboro, Tennessee 37133

Printed and Bound in the United States of America

Contents

Chapter 1
That's My Crowd
Part I

"Running with the crowd" is a catchphrase with overwhelmingly negative overtones. So often on any given day the crowds about you are probably "running" the wrong way. It does therefore behoove all of us to pay attention to where we have intimate fellowship and with whom we unite in partnership. In other words, we need to think carefully about "the crowd" with whom we align and with whom we associate ourselves.

Let's review a few biblical principles in this consideration:

(1) Proverbs 1:10–16:

"My son, if sinners entice thee, consent thou not.

"If they say, Come with us, let us lay wait for blood, let us lurk privily for the innocent without cause:

"Let us swallow them up alive as the grave; and whole, as those that go down into the pit:

"We shall find all precious substance, we shall fill our houses with spoil:

"Cast in thy lot among us; let us all have one purse:

"My son, walk not thou in the way with them; refrain thy foot from their path:

"For their feet run to evil, and make haste to shed blood."

(2) Proverbs 9:6:

"Forsake the foolish, and live."

(3) Proverbs 13:20:

"He that walketh with wise men shall be wise: but a companion of fools shall be destroyed."

1

(4) Proverbs 14:7:

"Go from the presence of a foolish man, when thou perceivest not in him the lips of knowledge."

(5) Proverbs 15:6:

"In the house of the righteous is much treasure: but in the revenues of the wicked is trouble."

(6) Proverbs 17:1:

"Better is a dry morsel, and quietness therewith, than an house full of sacrifices with strife."

(7) Proverbs 18:5:

"It is not good to accept the person of the wicked, to overthrow the righteous in judgment."

(8) Proverbs 19:4, 6–7:

"Wealth maketh many friends; but the poor is separated from his neighbour."

"Many will intreat the favour of the prince: and every man is a friend to him that giveth gifts.

"All the brethren of the poor do hate him: how much more do his friends go far from him? he pursueth them with words, yet they are wanting to him."

(9) Proverbs 20:19:

"He that goeth about as a talebearer revealeth secrets: therefore meddle not with him that flattereth with his lips."

(Other Scriptures will be listed at the outset of Parts II and III of this series.)

Clearly, the Word of God reveals the importance of our friendships and our fellowship! The crowd with whom we choose to fraternize can have a major impact on us and all we hold dear. These passages repeatedly advise and command us to be discerning, to be deliberate and to be dutiful in our associations.

When we know the will of God, we should choose it and do it! When we can figure what is good, then it is right and best to pursue it. When we find others who are obedient to God, we should run with them: they are the right crowd!

On the other hand, when the Word of God is treated lightly or shown disrespect, that's not the right crowd!

When the good and godly is dismissed as Victorian or puritanical, that's not the right crowd!

When we see others headed off to do their own thing without a yieldedness to the Word of God, that's not the right crowd!

Choosing "your crowd" may not always be easy. It may be, in fact, perplexing, even to the point of confusing!

You may not have all the issues figured out, and you may be tempted to take a "so what?" attitude and do nothing, as do so many others. But I hope you will have the maturity not to take the easy route and the discernment to keep attentive to the issues.

It is my heartfelt desire to be a blessing and help you in any way I can. Let me tell you about the crowd with whom I've chosen to cast my lot.

Perhaps you too will decide "That's My Crowd!"

I. The Unchangeable God Crowd!

"For I am the LORD, I change not."—Mal. 3:6.

Consider, please, who God is and who is God!

The God who is the "God in heaven" (Dan. 2:28) is the One who "in the beginning...created the heaven and the earth" (Gen. 1:1).

(1) He is the triune, tripartite tri-unity, the Trinity—namely, God who is called Father; God the Son, Jesus Christ; and God the Holy Ghost.

(2) He is known by His Bible names and titles: Jehovah, Adonai (Lord), Elohim (God), the Most High God, the Almighty God, the Everlasting God, the Lord of Hosts, the Lord our Righteousness, the Lord our Peace, the Lord our Shepherd.

(3) He is distinguished by His place and position! Specifically and especially, He is both Creator and Redeemer. Out of nothing He, by His spoken word, commanded into existence planets, moons, stars, the animals, the plants and, yes, human life.

The God who is God is not made with human hands, but He is

the God who made every human hand. He is not some abstract idea or philosophic invention of the human mind. He sits astride the universe as its Maker and its Master! Knowing that the prize of His creation was a mere human, He thoughtfully, lovingly and wonderfully planned from the start to be Redeemer as well as Creator.

In the Old Testament the hints, the signs, the symbols, the types and the prophecies of the Lord Jesus Christ, the Saviour, are woven into the fabric of every page and paragraph. Ultimately, there was a time in history in which "the Word was made flesh, and dwelt among us, (and we beheld his glory, the glory as of the only begotten of the Father,) full of grace and truth" (John 1:14).

The angel of the Lord, Heaven's herald of the great event, declared: "I bring you good tidings of great joy, which shall be to all people. For unto you is born this day in the city of David a Saviour, which is Christ the Lord" (Luke 2:10–11). Thus, the Great Creator is also our Redeemer!

(4) He is recognizable by His character and His characteristics: He is omnipotent (all powerful); omniscient (all knowing); omnipresent (everywhere present at the same time); eternal (no beginning and no end); holy (perfect and flawless); immutable (unchangeable); infinite; sovereign; and unsearchable.

The God who is God is NOT Allah! He is NOT Baal! NOT Molech! NOT Pithom! NOT Diana of Ephesus! Not any of them! Not at all! Not in the least!

Now, let me say that my God is "the unchangeable God" and the crowd that is "my crowd" is acquainted with Him, aligned with Him and attached to Him! Amen! "That's My Crowd!"

II. The Unmistakable Jesus Crowd!

(Gen. 3:15; Isa. 7:14; 9:6; Micah 5:2; Matt. 1:18–25; John 1:17, 29; Acts 2:36; 4:12; Phil. 2:5–11; Col. 1:12–19; II John 9; Rev. 1:1–2, 5, 7, 17–18)

He is the subject of Old Testament prophecy and the central character of the New Testament: the virgin-born, sinless, only begotten Son of God, and God the Son—He is fully deity and fully human. He who has always been, was made flesh at Bethlehem; died on the cross as the substitute for us; paid the debt for our sins and triumphantly arose from the grave; ascended to Heaven (literally, bodily and visibly); and is someday returning to earth (literally, bodily and visibly) to rule and reign for a thousand years as King of Kings and Lord of Lords and will, as the eternal King, take all His ransomed home to Heaven.

He is not just a prophet but greater than all the prophets (Matt. 12:41); more than a teacher or preacher, He is the great God Himself incarnate (John 1:1–5, 14), of whom it is said, "We have not an high priest which cannot be touched with the feeling of our infirmities; but was in all points tempted like as we are, yet without sin" (Heb. 4:15).

The Lord Jesus Christ is the central figure of our faith. He is Messiah, Saviour, Lord and Master. We who serve Him defer to Him in all things, exalt Him above all others and give Him first and full place in our lives and work.

The crowd that is "our crowd" is energized and elated by the Person of Jesus Christ! We are excited by who He is, what He says, how He directs, where He leads and when He returns.

We have not forgotten that we are forgiven, saved, born again, justified, redeemed, regenerated, secured forever and Heaven-bound because of Him. The folks who are by faith serving the Saviour, "this same Jesus" (Acts 1:11), the unmistakable Jesus—they are the ones with whom I have kinship! Amen! "That's My Crowd!"

III. The Unedited Bible Crowd!

"All scripture is given by inspiration of God, and is profitable for doctrine, for reproof, for correction, for instruction in righteousness."— II Tim. 3:16.

(Ps. 12:6–7; 33:4; 119:1–176; Prov. 30:5; Isa. 8:16; 28:13; 34:16; 40:8; 55:10–11; Jer. 23:29; Mark 13:31; II Cor. 4:2; II Tim. 3:15–17; Heb. 4:12; I Pet. 1:23–25; II Pet. 1:19–21)

There was a time not so long ago when the Bible was the Bible and not just a "version" of it. But in the past hundred years or so, and especially the last fifty years, first one and then another have come out with "their versions."

Very often "the versions" have been motivated by bias or bucks!

Either way, it is a formula for manipulating the text to someone's advantage.

Most of the "new versions" are translated from a corrupt text! In the 1880s Westcott and Hort tampered with the Greek text to the tune of 9,970 additions, subtractions or emendations. It is the Westcott-Hort text that has invariably been the choice of today's Bible translation committees. How on earth can they expect to have a good English version that is rendered from such a tampered-with text?

When I became an independent Baptist in 1976, everybody was packing a King James Bible! It was, and had been for almost four centuries, the undisputed, authoritative, standard English text! It is still the standard which all "the versions" are trying to outdo!

The cults, the neo-religious scholars, the worldly church folks and the liberal-influenced pulpiteers of the past decades have tried every scheme imaginable to "undo" the Grand Old Book that has served us so well.

I know it's strong, it's bold, it's piercing to the heart, it's confrontational to sinners, it's not cozy with the culture, and it doesn't read like a newspaper (thankfully). I'm well aware of its Elizabethan-style English and all the complaints about the "thee's" and "thou's." But after all, it's the Bible—distinctive, decisive and dynamic! Amen!

When you change "Bibles" frequently or make place for whatever "new Bible" is just off the press, you will soon discover you and your people will be unsure whether or not you have the Word of God at all! You will be meeting to dissect and debate it, voting in committee on whether this or that is true; and all of you will walk away weakened, wishy-washy and without an authoritative text!

In recent times more and more independent and fundamental folks are becoming enamored with some "new version" because "it is so much easier for us to understand." Strange, isn't it, that the most highly educated generation in history supposedly has trouble "understanding" what everybody read and enjoyed without a hitch just a few years back! Wise up, folks; there's more to it than they led you to believe!

Some will criticize my appeal for "an unedited Bible" by saying that this is a new idea, it is an extremist position, and it was not this kind of an issue even a generation ago. In response, let me offer two things—namely, results and research:

(1) Results! We've had time now to see and to evaluate what happens when there is no standard text! The results for individual Christians and for churches are not good! The historical track record ought to be testimony abundant and sufficient!

(2) Research! The past fifty years the text issue has had more extensive study given to it than in all the centuries prior! After all, the clamor to change the Bible did not gain momentum until recent years. The pressure of such events has forced a lot of people to look more closely than ever and thus prepare themselves to defend the Word of God!

So, I'm not bashful to say that I'm ill at ease with the "Bible editors." The crowd that I joined in 1976 was enthusiastically packing and preaching a King James Bible! An unedited Bible! Amen! "That's My Crowd!"

IV. The Unrevokable Salvation Crowd!

"For God so loved the world, that he gave his only begotten Son, that whosoever believeth in him should not perish, but have everlasting life."—John 3:16.

(John 1:12; 3:16–18; 6:47; 10:28–29; I John 5:11–13; Jude 24–25)

The salvation that God gives is full, free and forever! We believe and preach the eternal security of the believer, sometimes referred to as "once saved, always saved." If you have something religious that can be received and lost, I assure you it is not the salvation of God! You don't get saved by your performance, and you don't lose your salvation by the failure to perform. Some teach that salvation is received *by grace through faith,* but (they say) if you don't do certain works, or (some even say) if you sin, then you lose salvation! Such reasoning is flawed. It has no scriptural basis! It is a sinister, satanic trick—utter nonsense!

All of us are sinners! God has provided salvation for us through the *full payment* of Christ's death, burial and resurrection (I Cor. 15:3–4). When we place our faith (trust) in Christ as Saviour, He does truly save us and awards us everlasting life (John 3:36).

7

We are at the same time *birthed* into the family of God (John 3:3; Gal. 3:26). We will then be preserved (Jude 1) by the Lord Jesus Christ—making our salvation totally dependent upon Him (Jude 24).

Therefore, the sustaining of our salvation does not hinge upon *our perseverance,* but instead, it is held firmly by *His preservation!*

So, the salvation we have and the salvation we preach is unrevokable! The crowd that is "my crowd" preaches that "once for all" (Heb. 10:10) salvation! Amen! "That's My Crowd!"

V. The Unforgettable Heritage Crowd!

Remember *"the rock whence ye are hewn"* (Isa. 51:1).

It's almost as if a lot of folks who once were "our crowd" are now adrift on the open seas. Wherever the current winds of culture and popularity blow, that's where they sail! They redefine terms! They change their approach! They group themselves with others not of "our crowd"! Of course, all of this is done with constant reminders of "this is not the 1970s; this is the twenty-first century"; "you've got to change or you'll die"; "nobody does that anymore"; and an assortment of other like-spirited clichés designed to shame us and tame us!

Their rallying cry is a twofold mantra borrowed from the dead-in-the-water "neo's," namely, "Let's all get together," and "It's time we stop fighting one another." Such naiveté is beyond belief! It's neither the fabric nor the fiber from which the fundamentalist was carved.

Our fundamental crowd has always "gotten together" around our principles and our practices! We've always remained "separate" from those whose ministry was not of similar convictions! We "get together" often—but it's in gatherings where the like-minded are featured in the pulpit and classroom.

To hear some of them talk, you would think independent Baptists are the only people who ever disagree! They either don't know about or choose to ignore the self-styled "holy war" in the Southern Baptist Convention that started in 1979 and continues even now! Perhaps they don't read the denominational journals of the Methodists, the Presbyterians, the Lutherans, the Episcopalians (as I do) and see the constant quarreling that goes on.

The great fellowships of the independent Baptist movement were all born out of conflict. When great issues were at stake, they stood up to be counted! It is our heritage!

When we ponder the legacy of John R. Rice, Curtis Hutson, Lester Roloff, Lee Roberson, Tom Malone, J. Frank Norris, Harold Sightler, Bob Jones, Sr., G. B. Vick, B. R. Lakin, Jack Hyles, Harvey Springer, Myron Cedarholm, Monroe Parker, T. T. Shields, Charles Spurgeon, Oliver B. Greene and others, we cannot but rejoice for their faith, their stand, their boldness, their tenacity, their witness, their testimony, their convictions and their courage! What a heritage we have! Amen! "That's My Crowd!"

VI. The Unalterable Fundamental Crowd!

"If thou put the brethren in remembrance of these things, thou shalt be a good minister of Jesus Christ, nourished up in the words of faith and of good doctrine, whereunto thou hast attained.

"But refuse profane and old wives' fables, and exercise thyself rather unto godliness."—I Tim. 4:6–7.

(Col. 2:8; II Tim. 1:13; 2:10–14; 4:1–5; Titus 2:1; Heb. 13:9; II Pet. 1:12; 2:1–3; 3:1–2, 17)

Because the liberal American news media has done an ongoing hatchet job on the term *fundamental*, some have suggested we employ some different term to describe ourselves. Worse yet, some are twisting the term with definitions that are more appeasing and more appealing to the popular culture!

But here's where we are! We are not charismatic! Not Pentecostal! We are not "evangelical"! We are not cultists! We are not Catholic! We are not Promise Keepers! We are not ecumenists! We are by profession, by precept and by practice *fundamentalists!* By that, we mean we believe the Bible! We accept it literally at face value! We like what we find in the Bible, and so we build our lives and ministries around it! In other words, "fundamentalism" is just basic New Testament Christianity!

We believe all of us should cling tenaciously to "the old paths" of our Faith—the teaching and philosophy so clearly evident in the Bible. Further, we believe we should stay a little more than arm's length from others (even Christians) who do not do likewise.

If a church, a fellowship or a convention has employees or missionaries that are known to be liberals, we do not believe they should be supported from the Sunday offerings! Church money should never (in any amount) be used to support such foolishness, but it happens all the time. It ought not so to be!

"My crowd" declares itself fundamental and distinguishes itself to be so by separating from any and all who are otherwise engaged.

I thank God for the dear servants of God who are unashamed of our heritage, unimpressed with today's neo-environment, and who are excitedly and unalterably fundamentalist in what they believe, where they stand, and whom they support! Amen! "That's My Crowd!"

VII. The Unambiguous Doctrine Crowd!

(Matt. 16:12; Acts 2:42; Rom. 16:17; Gal. 1:6–12; Eph. 4:14; I Tim. 1:3, 10; 4:13–16; II Tim. 4:2–3)

Doctrine is a dirty word to a lot of religious folks these days, but let me remind you, it is a good Bible word! The ecumenical philosophers say, "Doctrine divides." For once, they are right! It divides truth from error, good from evil, right from wrong, sheep from goats, etc. In the kitchen, at the pharmacy and at the hospital, I hope somebody has the conviction and the courage to separate the wheat from the chaff. Amen? With eternal issues at stake, the diligence should be no less intense at the church house!

You hear them say things like, "Well, everybody gets something different out of the Bible." It's like God could not make Himself clear enough for us to read the Book and come up with the truth! But they're wrong to suggest such a thing! The Bible is clear on so many things. We can therefore preach and teach Bible doctrine without ambiguity: (1) an inerrant, infallible, authoritative, reliable Bible; (2) the Father, Son and Holy Ghost—the Trinity; (3) the virgin birth, the vicarious atonement and the victorious resurrection of Christ; (4) salvation by grace through faith; (5) creation, not evolution; (6) a literal Heaven and a literal Hell; (7) baptism of believers—after salvation; (8) premillennial, pretribulational second coming; (9) ecclesiastical separation; (10) personal separation and holy living; and more!

Unambiguous doctrine! Amen! "That's My Crowd!"

In the next two chapters, I will continue with the theme of this essay on "That's My Crowd!" When it is finished, I believe the issue will be pretty clear that: (1) associations do matter; (2) running with the right crowd is important; and (3) there are some clear-cut principles about how to identify "your crowd." In these days of compromise, it is vital that we know who we are and run with a crowd of which we can enthusiastically say, "That's My Crowd!"

Chapter 2

That's My Crowd
Part II

In our consideration of "the crowd" with whom we cast our lot and in carefully acclaiming, "That's my crowd," it is noteworthy that numerous Bible principles do appropriate themselves to the subject. So much that is wrong can be avoided if we hear and heed the clearly revealed truth of Scripture. Likewise, things which are right are more easily discern if we know what the Lord has said about them.

Ponder now these verses which teach us things about the company we keep:

"The righteous man wisely considereth the house of the wicked...."

"The man that wandereth out of the way of understanding shall remain in the congregation of the dead."—Prov. 21:12, 16.

"Cast out the scorner, and contention shall go out; yea, strife and reproach shall cease."

"Make no friendship with an angry man; and with a furious man thou shalt not go:

"Lest thou learn his ways, and get a snare to thy soul."

"Remove not the ancient landmark, which thy fathers have set."—Prov. 22:10, 24–25, 28.

"Eat thou not the bread of him that hath an evil eye, neither desire thou his dainty meats."

"Let not thine heart envy sinners: but be thou in the fear of the LORD all the day long."

"Be not among winebibbers; among riotous eaters of flesh."—Prov. 23:6, 17, 20.

"Be not thou envious against evil men, neither desire to be with them."

"For by wise counsel thou shalt make thy war: and in multitude of counsellors there is safety."

"My son, fear thou the LORD and the king: and meddle not with them that are given to change:

"For their calamity shall rise suddenly; and who knoweth the ruin of them both?"—Prov. 24:1, 6, 21–22.

In the first chapter, I gave seven defining elements by which I believe you can identify us. They are: The Unchangeable God Crowd, The Unmistakable Jesus Crowd, The Unedited Bible Crowd, The Unrevokable Salvation Crowd, The Unforgettable Heritage Crowd, The Unalterable Fundamental Crowd, The Unambiguous Doctrine Crowd.

Now here are seven additional items which will further clarify the case I'm making here:

VIII. The Unashamedly Local Church Crowd!

"And I say also unto thee, That thou art Peter, and upon this rock I will build my church; and the gates of hell shall not prevail against it."— Matt. 16:18.

(Col. 1:18; I Thess. 5:12–13; I Tim. 5:17; Heb. 13:7, 17, 24)

Every individual local assembly of baptized believers bound together in a body and organized for the work of the ministry is a church. When we talk about "the church," we are either referring to a particular local church or to the church as an institution.

Every Christian should be active in a local church. You cannot fulfill the mandates of Christ and the duties of the Christian life apart from partnership and fellowship with others of like faith and like-minded believers in a local church.

When the ecumenists and their disciples talk about "the larger body or the whole body" in reference to the church, they are off the mark. Everyone who is saved is in God's family, but that is not synonymous with "the church."

I am unashamedly a *local church* advocate! When the work of God has been done through the years, it has almost always been done directly through a local church or indirectly as a product of the energies of local church pastors and people pulling together to spearhead a common effort (for example, mission boards, colleges, the Sword, etc.).

We believe in *the local church*. The folks who are anti-local-church usually have their own predetermined and often self-serving agenda. That anti-church spirit is often a rebellion against authority. It is not a spirit with which we ought to link up.

The crowd that's thinking straight about church intends to serve the Lord honorably and magnify Him in all its ministry. "Unto him be glory in the church by Christ Jesus throughout all ages, world without end. Amen" (Eph. 3:21).

Amen! "That's my crowd!"

IX. The Undisputably Separatist Crowd!

In recent times several well-intentioned men have said to me that they believe we should separate from nonbelievers but that we should not do so from professing believers. I believe they are only half right. There is, in my view, sufficient biblical admonition to separate also from fellow believers over significant issues. So let me get some scriptural documentation before us which should help clear this up: Romans 16:17–18; I Corinthians 1:10; II Corinthians 6:14–7:1; II Corinthians 11:13–15; Ephesians 5:7,11; II Thessalonians 3:6,11,14–15.

"Now we command you, brethren, in the name of our Lord Jesus Christ, that ye withdraw yourselves from every brother that walketh disorderly, and not after the tradition which he received of us."—II Thess. 3:6.

Separation is the very antithesis, the exact opposite, of ecumenism.

Even casual readers of the Bible should see quickly that separation is a decidedly scriptural teaching.

Some passages admonish the matter of personal separation (issues of holiness, sanctification, lifestyle); and others address the issue of ecclesiastical separation. We believe that this doctrine of separation is a landmark of faith and a watermark of fundamentalism.

It's easy to go with the cultural flow, ignore the doctrinal errors and worldly lifestyle and be in fellowship with anything and everything.

That is the way most people prefer to go these days, but we believe the Bible instructs otherwise.

A lot of people misunderstand the concept of separation. Some have said we are judging people's salvation. That's not true at all. None of us can judge whether or not someone else is saved. We can, however, see and hear the issues of doctrine, lifestyle and ministry. This is what separation addresses.

Others seem to think we mean that you can have no one in your church unless he or she agrees with you on everything. That's ridiculous, of course. It would be impossible to effect even if you tried. Every church that is reaching out as it should has all kinds of folks in all stages of development sitting in the pews. Thankfully, they are there. We would not want it any other way. After they are saved, they should be taught Bible truths on everything (Matt. 28:20). Indeed, the teaching of sanctification, purity and holiness will ultimately affect their lifestyle.

When folks want to preach, sing, teach, etc., they should be willing to meet scriptural qualifications and whatever standards may be appropriate. The platform of leadership is the sum and substance of the ecclesiastical separation debate. It is only right that such standards be adopted and adhered to by the workers in the church. Go anyplace in town (McDonald's, Wendy's, Sears—anywhere), inquire about employment, and you'll discover quickly they all have standards. How utterly unthinkable for the churches to take an "every-man-do-what's-right-in-his-own-eyes approach"!

Should we have speakers on our platform who are liberals? Should we have conservative speakers who knowingly support liberals from their Sunday offerings? Should we have on our platform speakers who are affiliated with groups who retain liberals on their payrolls? Should we have on our platforms speakers who are worldly and carnal in their presentation and their lifestyle? Should we have on our platform speakers who run with and speak for groups such as Promise Keepers, TBN, Campus Crusade, the SBC, etc.?

The answer to all the foregoing five questions is a big, strong "NO!" Naturally, there will be numerous folks, including some of our brethren, who disagree. But we believe our position on separation is scriptural, seasoned and sensible. The separatist crowd—"that's my crowd!" Amen!

X. The Untiring Soul-Winning Crowd!

"And daily in the temple, and in every house, they ceased not to teach and preach Jesus Christ."—Acts 5:42.

(Ps. 126:5–6; Prov. 11:30; Dan. 12:3; Matt. 28:18–20; Acts 1:8; Rom. 9:1–3; 10:1–4; Rev. 22:17)

Jesus said that He Himself came "to seek and to save that which was lost" (Luke 19:10). In the same clear voice with which He defined His own agenda, He laid out very carefully what He had in mind for those of us who follow Him: "As my Father hath sent me, even so send I you" (John 20:21).

The decision to follow Christ should be understood not in the levity of our self-centered expectations but in the light of His own declaration: "Follow me, and I will make you fishers of men" (Matt. 4:19). It's simple, really: If you follow, you fish! If you're not fishing, you're not following! Folks, let's get this settled: Jesus intends for you to be a soul winner!

Our crowd is the soul-winning crowd! Untiringly and unceasingly we are going after sinners to get them saved. Fifty-two weeks a year, seven days a week—no letup! Every week people in sight of church houses are dying and going to Hell. We cannot justify our yawning attitude. We must not give in to the pressure of schedules, critics, circumstances or anything else. The pursuit of souls is not an option: it is a matter of obedience! The soul winners—"that's my crowd!" Amen!

XI. The Unintimidated Preaching Crowd!

(Matt. 10:7; Mark 16:15; Rom. 10:14–15; I Cor. 1:23; Eph. 3:8; II Tim. 4:2)

There is a place in the church for teaching, and there is also a place for preaching! Teaching instructs; preaching instructs and inspires! Teaching educates; preaching educates, expounds, exposes, exhorts, evangelizes, enlists and energizes!

While the popular venues remove the pulpit; dress down the preacher; speak in low-voice, conversational tones; address psychological subjects; lull you to sleep with counseling jargon; avoid all rhetoric which appears confrontational and make only token use of the Bible, they are not the crowd that is my crowd! My crowd is led by preachers who are unafraid and unapologetically committed to preaching.

The preacher who is a preacher knows that he has a mandate from God, that he is authorized to stand up and speak for God, that he is unmistakably a man of God. He preaches not himself, but Christ; not his word, but God's Word; not religion, but regeneration; not reformation, but righteousness; and not the wishes of the culture, but the will of God!

Preaching is authoritative! Preaching is bold! Preaching is convicting! Preaching is defining! Preaching is enthusiastic! Preaching is fervent! Preaching is God-centered!

Preaching brings heat and light. It attends the issues. It stands courageously in the face of a godless culture. It explains what's right and what's wrong.

Preaching asks for a verdict. Just as it communicates the message of truth, so it calls for a decision. It asks the hearer to respond and do the bidding of God. That's preaching—and that's the way my crowd goes about things!

When you hear people making light of preaching and diminishing the place of the preacher, you do well to watch out: it's likely a harbinger of unacceptable things on the horizon.

Preaching! Yes, we believe in preaching! We love preaching! Amen! "That's my crowd!"

XII. The Uncompromising Music Crowd!

No jump! No jiggle! No jazz! No jive! No rock 'n' roll! No hip-hop! No rap! No Broadway, no Hollywood, no Nashville, no Branson!

Music in the church ought to be distinctively Christian in its message, its manner and its motive!

The subject and the substance of the song either make it or break it. It should be focused on a gospel and/or doctrinal theme. It should be decidedly biblical.

The style of the song's presentation should not mirror worldly performers. It should maximize the message of the song. The singer is a human instrument, and God does use us to be His mouthpiece. We must work to be sure, however, that the music is more about

Him than it is about us. Style should not be about culture. *"My music"* is usually a faulty approach to doing *Christian* music.

The pastor of every local church should maintain control of the music department (just as with everything else in the church). He should have full say-so on all music at all church functions, including veto power (without committee approval).

The world offers a smorgasbord of music which some religious folks cannot resist imitating! It is a sad day when the church house is filled with the same sounds that fill the nightclub down the street. There should be no mistaking the musical testimony of God's people from the noisy rattling of the worldly performers. The sound and the substance of Christian music should be distinctive.

XIII. The Unwavering Standards Crowd!

(Rom. 13:9,13; I. Cor. 9:26–27; 10:23,31–33; 16:13; Eph. 5:1–7; 6:11–18)

Standards? "Oh no!" the critics cry. "You're a legalist!" Let me say firmly yet kindly: that's an unwarranted, libelous and deliberate slander of the truth!

When a preacher tries to twist the message of Galatians to fit his casual lifestyle, he often rails at the fundamental crowd with an accusation of legalism. He's not only a false accuser when he does that, but he is also distorting and misusing the Scripture! Let me explain.

If a person tries to use works (any works) *in order to receive or maintain* salvation, then I agree that he is a legalist. By mandating works as a condition upon which salvation is received, he is way off base. No man can receive or retain salvation by his own performance. To attempt to do so is a faulty view of the Bible plan of salvation. I personally do not know of even one fundamental preacher who preaches works as a condition of salvation. Therefore, I do not know even one fundamental preacher who is a legalist!

But after salvation is received, works are a factor in the Christian life (Eph. 2:10). Our works are *because of* our salvation. They are the fruit (not the root) of salvation.

So we believe it is right that a church require certain standards of its leadership (I Tim. 3:1–12; Titus 1:5–9). Are we legalists because we insist that the pastor and deacons be biblically qualified to serve in office? I don't think so. It is just right to do it.

Furthermore, we believe it is right for the pastor to preach standards and require that workers in the church exhibit enough spiritual maturity to set an example for the unsaved and for 'the weaker brethren' (I Cor. 8:11–13).

Therefore, we believe Christians should:

(1) not drink alcohol (Prov. 20:1);

(2) not smoke or use drugs (Rom. 6:13–14; I Cor. 6:19–20);

(3) have clean mouths (Eph. 4:29);

(4) stay clear of enticements to do evil (Phil. 4:8; I Thess. 5:22);

(5) groom themselves appropriately (I Cor. 11:13–15; I Tim. 2:9–10; I Pet. 3:3–4).

Folks, this is not unreasonable—and it is NOT legalism! It's what we all did just a short while ago.

Oddly enough, even those who cry "legalism" also have some standards; they're just lower ones!

Standards! Yes, indeed! Amen! "That's my crowd!"

XIV. The Undaunted Vision Crowd!

(Prov. 29:18; Rom. 1:14–16; II Cor. 4:1; Gal. 6:9–10; II Thess. 3:1,13; II Tim. 2:1–10; I John 3:2; Rev. 22:17)

The mentality of our crowd is not "wait and see" or status quo. It is not fear that motivates us, but faith! We see a world seemingly bent on destroying itself, and we believe that many of those aimless souls plundering blindly toward eternity can be reached and won.

It's true that the cults and isms of a thousand varieties are ensnaring multitudes, but our God-given, scripturally defined vision is undaunted.

We believe God! We believe the Bible! We believe the faith of our fathers should be the faith of our future. While the world changes constantly, the tenets of Faith are steady and unmovable.

The mandate of God to His children to love Him and serve Him, to win souls and get the Gospel to the whole world is the driving compulsion of our souls. The blur of activity, the pressure of our adversaries and the clamor of our critics do not dim our vision for one moment.

The trends and the polls do not set our agenda for us. The whims of a godless culture and the worldly mind-set of the religious mainstream do not deter us nor discourage us.

Our doctrine is settled! Our duty is our program. Our direction is fixed.

Yes, there are preachers and other Christian workers across the world whose vision is undaunted! Amen! "That's my crowd!"

Conclusion of Chapter II

So, let me reiterate the appeals I've made thus far about "my crowd." They are: The Unchangeable God Crowd, The Unmistakable Jesus Crowd, The Unedited Bible Crowd, The Unrevokable Salvation Crowd, The Unforgettable Heritage Crowd, The Unalterable Fundamental Crowd, The Unambiguous Doctrine Crowd, The Unashamedly Local Church Crowd, The Undisputably Separatist Crowd, The Untiring Soul-Winning Crowd, The Unintimidated Preaching Crowd, The Uncompromising Music Crowd, The Unwavering Standards Crowd, The Undaunted Vision Crowd.

By the elements thus far presented we are defined and we are identified. It is who we are and what we are. It also helps to explain why we are the way we are.

I'm excited about it too! Yes, I am thrilled to the depths of my soul because there's still "a crowd" like what I'm describing.

Chapter 3

That's My Crowd
Part III

All people have friends with whom they associate. Some may be only casual acquaintances. Others may be very close, intimate friends.

In the ministry, we all work diligently to establish friendships for the sake of the Gospel and for the ministry, as well as for our personal lives. It is right to do so, and it is profitable in so many ways.

The Bible says, "A man that hath friends must shew himself friendly" (Prov. 18:24). It also says, "By this shall all men know that ye are my disciples, if ye have love one to another" (John 13:35). These are great passages with great truths, and we hold them dear. Unfortunately, they are often quoted in such a way as to suggest that they are the primary and exclusive mandates of the Bible.

When we take a stand for clearly revealed Bible truths, it doesn't mean we are unloving. The Bible speaks as clearly about the issues of doctrine and separation as it does about love. To quote only the love passages is simply not an honest usage of the Scripture. We have a responsibility, I believe, to look at the whole picture and not merely one selected portion.

Consider now these passages as they relate to our associations and our relationships:

"Take away the dross from the silver, and there shall come forth a vessel for the finer.

"Take away the wicked from before the king, and his throne shall be established in righteousness."

"Confidence in an unfaithful man in time of trouble is like a broken tooth, and a foot out of joint."

23

"It is better to dwell in the corner of the housetop, than with a brawling woman and in a wide house."

"A righteous man falling down before the wicked is as a troubled fountain, and a corrupt spring."—Prov. 25:4–5, 19, 24, 26.

"The legs of the lame are not equal: so is a parable in the mouth of fools."—Prov. 26:7.

"A prudent man foreseeth the evil, and hideth himself; but the simple pass on, and are punished."

"Iron sharpeneth iron; so a man sharpeneth the countenance of his friend."—Prov. 27:12, 17.

"They that forsake the law praise the wicked: but such as keep the law contend with them."

"Whoso keepeth the law is a wise son: but he that is a companion of riotous men shameth his father."—Prov. 28:4, 7.

"When the righteous are in authority, the people rejoice: but when the wicked beareth rule, the people mourn."

"If a wise man contendeth with a foolish man, whether he rage or laugh, there is no rest."

"Whoso is partner with a thief hateth his own soul: he heareth cursing, and bewrayeth it not."

"An unjust man is an abomination to the just: and he that is upright in the way is abomination to the wicked."—Prov. 29:2, 9, 24, 27.

Just ponder the principles in this great Book of God's Proverbs! How enlightening! How instructive! How important they are to us!

In the first two chapters, I said that my crowd is: The Unchangeable God Crowd, The Unmistakable Jesus Crowd, The Unedited Bible Crowd, The Unrevokable Salvation Crowd, The Unforgettable Heritage Crowd, The Unalterable Fundamental Crowd, The Unambiguous Doctrine Crowd, The Unashamedly Local Church Crowd, The Undisputably Separatist Crowd, The Untiring Soul-Winning Crowd, The Unintimidated Preaching Crowd, The Uncompromising Music Crowd, The Unwavering Standards Crowd, The Undaunted Vision Crowd.

Now here are seven additional matters which I believe to be a significant part of the crowd that's headed right:

XV. The Unceasing Prayer Crowd!
(Matt. 5:44; 6:7; 9:38; 26:41; Mark 11:24; I Tim. 2:8; Jas. 5:13–16)

"Pray without ceasing."—I Thess. 5:17.

The crowd that walks with God is a praying people. How can we wear His name and serve Him if we do not stay in touch with Him? Strange it is that Christians fume and fret, they figure every angle, and so often only as a last resort do they fling a prayer upward.

"Let us pray" should not be the invitation to recite some trite little formula with an "amen" on the end of it. It should be the warm, live and real expression of our heart and soul.

Dr. John R. Rice said, "Prayer is asking." As a people—fundamental, separated, soul-winning, Bible-believing people—we know we need the Lord to fill us, to feed us and to fight for us. So we pray! That is, we ask!

Prayer is not just for the closet where we are alone. It is for every step we take every moment of the day.

Because we take our Christian experience seriously, we are also serious in prayer. We cry out to God with our needs, our hurts, our burdens, our vision and our cares. We pray for our families and our friends. We pray for the churches. We pray for anointing and power. We pray for souls. We pray for victory. We pray—and often. We pray humbly, thankfully and expectantly.

"Let us therefore come boldly unto the throne of grace, that we may obtain mercy, and find grace to help in time of need."—Heb. 4:16.

Yes, the crowd with whom we identify is the unceasing prayer crowd. "That's My Crowd!" Amen!

XVI. The Unrelenting Revival Crowd!
(Ps. 85:6; Hab. 3:2; Acts 2:39–47; 4:31; Eph. 6:10–20; Phil. 1:8–11; I Thess. 5:1–11; II Tim. 4:3–5; Jas. 4:7–8; Rev. 2—3)

Some people seem clueless on this subject and express no knowledge of it or need for it. That's truly sad!

Others talk it incessantly, but no matter how much God blesses, they still act as though it is illusive to them. They're sincere, I think, but they're just talking—nothing more.

Then you have the folks who believe God is arbitrarily withholding blessing, stingy with His grace and unwilling to visit us in power. That is totally ridiculous!

So, let's dig out the truth (it's in the Book); let's talk about it (spread the Word); let's tell the Lord we want it (He's ready to give it); and let's taste it! Amen!

Mediocrity! Carnality! Wishy-washy! Running with the wrong crowds! Wimping our way through the Christian life! Letting our generation die and go to Hell without a witness! No way! Not today! Not ever! That's not the way "our crowd" behaves itself!

We want the blessing of God in its richness and fullness. We want it personally, and we want it in the work where we labor! So we yield ourselves to God; we surrender wholeheartedly to Him. It is an intimate and personal relationship upon which we base our lives and build our ministries. Because of our alignment with Him and our adoration for Him, we give full attention to His Word, His wisdom, His will and His way.

When other things, whether they be good or bad, diminish our love for Him and disengage us from our close personal walk with Him, then we need revival!

"Our crowd" is not happy unless we are walking with God! We preach, we sing, we pray, and we plead—and we want revival!

We're not chasing some new and foolish game plan that was hatched in committee—we want revival! We are unrelenting in our determination and our zeal to have it God's way. That's revival and "That's My Crowd!" Amen!

XVII. The Unshakable Family Crowd!

(Gen. 2:18, 21–25; Deut. 6:6–25; Josh. 24:15; Matt. 19:3–9; I Cor. 7:1–6; Eph. 5:21–6:4; I Tim. 5:1–16; Titus 2:1–8; I Pet. 3:1–7)

The family is the cornerstone upon which our society is built! The biblical model is one man and one woman in a monogamous relationship for a lifetime.

There are *no* same-sex unions in God's plan! Homosexuality is not only a biological and moral perversion, it is a satanic attack upon the family.

"Our crowd" is unapologetic and unintimidated about our advocacy for the traditional family. The man is to be the husband and the father. The woman is to be the wife and the mother. The children are to be the children! Amen!

The social engineers of the twenty-first century are attempting to redefine and reinvent the family. They hate God, and they hate the divine legislation. They do not intend to be boxed in morally and socially. Their disdain for those of us who insist upon a scriptural standard for the family is heady and hostile. For several decades they have methodically gone about the task of breaking down the family structure in preparation for the new game plan they are now attempting to implement (namely, same-sex unions, homosexual marriages, unrestrained sexual debauchery, etc.).

Unfortunately, the universities, the media, the courts, some religious groups and other influential elements of society have become partners with them in this madness.

But, thankfully, there are people stretching across a fairly broad spectrum who are not capitulating to this trend. Among the voices calling for sanity on this subject is this crowd that is "my crowd."

We believe that the Lord intended for men and women to honor their vows and rear their children in a godly manner. We are unshak-able in our convictions that the traditional family (as God designed it in Genesis) is the norm and ought to be a top priority for all of us. We also believe that we should be crying loudly against whatever elements are tearing out the foundations of the family! We believe we should shout aloud a resounding "NO" to whatever devils attack the sanctity of the home. Amen! "That's My Crowd!"

XVIII. The Unimpeachable Integrity Crowd!
(II Cor. 6:3–10; 7:2; 13:7–9; Gal. 6:3–4; Eph. 4:1,17–32; 5:3–4,7–15; Phil. 4:8–9; I Thess. 4:11–12; 5:22; I Tim. 1:19; Titus 2:7–9,12)

Integrity? Yes, we believe the servants of God should be people of integrity (sincere, honest, upright)!

If you are saved and you have not shed the shackles of your worldly identity, shame on you! You cannot serve God with any degree of effectiveness, and you cannot do much about getting other people saved if your testimony is tainted and scarred with an ongoing lack of integrity. Let me be specific:

(1) You ought to be morally clean! If you are professing the sunlight of Heaven but living in the shadows of Hell, you are not doing what you should. You should not have habits (namely, smoking, drinking, drugs, worldly music, dancing, etc.) that would betray your testimony. If you are single, you should be sexually celibate. If you are married, you should be intensely faithful to your spouse and uphold without compromise the vows you made before God at the marriage altar! Amen!

(2) You ought to pay your debts! There is a whimsical carelessness about this among a large number of Christians. As unthinkable as it seems, some churches as well have debts they owe and about which they are doing nothing (except running and hiding). It is appalling! When you make a debt, pay it! If you get in a bind, go to the debtor and ask for a rearrangement of the payments; but do not allow yourself to have outstanding debts for which you have not taken full responsibility!

(3) You ought to tell the truth! Lying is not a spiritual or a Christian practice. It is rampant with some people in Christian circles. No wonder the testimony you bear yields no fruit. If you can't get your heart anchored to the truth, your lips will soon betray you in carnality!

Sure, we should preach the truth about creation, salvation, the Bible, etc.; but how about telling the truth about what you ate for breakfast and other such mundane things? It's integrity to do so!

Yes, integrity! Unimpeachable integrity! Amen! "That's My Crowd!"

XIX. The Unapologetically Premillennial Crowd!
(Acts 1:11; Phil. 3:20–21; I Thess. 4:13—5:10; II Thess. 1:7—2:12; Titus 2:13; II Pet. 2—3; Rev. 1—22)

"Maranatha" was a common greeting, salutation, in New Testament times. It is the Greek word that means "the Lord is coming." We believe, as did they, that the "same Jesus" who came the first time to provide redemption for us will come a second time to rapture His redeemed and take us home to Heaven with Him.

Although several schools of thought have developed on this, we believe the truth of the New Testament is what is known as the premillennial, pretribulational return of Christ. Here is a basic sketch of the details:

One of these days without any further announcement, the trumpet of Heaven will sound, and Jesus will come to catch out of the earth (rapture) the saved. He will come in the air, hover over the earth and snatch away every blood-bought believer. The bodies of the dead in Christ will be resurrected, and the saved who are still living will go to meet Him in the air. He will lead that great throng back to Heaven for the judgment seat of Christ (where rewards will be handed out) and the marriage supper of the Lamb.

When the saved are gone from earth, a period of seven years will unfold, bringing the greatest era of calamity the world has ever known. It is the Tribulation Period, the Great Tribulation! During that time, a one-world government and a one-world church will operate together under the dictatorial domain of the Antichrist. At the end of that era, the Lord Jesus and the raptured host of Heaven will emerge as a great army to wage war (Armageddon) against Satan, the Antichrist and their followers. We will win! Satan will be cast into Hell.

The great white throne judgment will be held to assign the degree of punishment to the unsaved multitudes who are headed for Hell. At the end of Armageddon, the Lord and His army will set up a kingdom on earth for a thousand years of His glorious reign as King of Kings and Lord of Lords. Finally, we will go home to Heaven to stay.

All of this could start anytime! We do not know when, but we know it could be any minute! We believe His coming is imminent. That's not to declare it is immediate, but obviously, it could be!

The crowd that's preaching the premillennial, pretribulational rapture—"That's My Crowd!" Amen!

XX. The Unmovable Stand Crowd!

(Jer. 6:16; I Cor. 15:58; 16:13; Eph. 6:11,13; II Tim. 2:19; 3:14–17; 4:2; Jude 3)

So many churches today are not voices for God but echoes of the times, the trends and the polls. Prophets who stand up tall and straight and thunder loudly the timeless, unchanging message of God are rare. Pulpiteers are often mere puppets answerable to a board, a committee or headquarters somewhere!

In "our crowd" the preachers are still men (male gender); and they are men of God (fervent about the truth which has been entrusted to them). They may have to move their furniture, but they will not move their convictions!

> Stand up, stand up for Jesus, ye
> soldiers of the cross!
> Lift high His royal banner; it must
> not suffer loss.
> From vict'ry unto vict'ry His army
> shall He lead
> Till ev'ry foe is vanquished and
> Christ is Lord indeed!

That great anthem is more than poetry set to music; it is for us a battle cry!

We preach the Bible stories about the Philistines of the Old Testament and the Pharisees of the New Testament; and while we are at it, we scold and scald the perverts and the polecats running up and down the Main Streets in our towns.

We believe abortion is wicked, and we say so!

We believe homosexuality is an abomination, and we say so!

We believe immorality in any venue is sin, and we say so!

We believe pornography is a social cancer, and we say so!

We oppose Hollywood, the ACLU, the PAW, the NOW, the NEA, the liberal AUSCS, the liberal politicians, the apostate clergy, the left-wing religious groups and whatever else shows up at the edge of town with poison to peddle.

There's no conflict between a strong soul-winning witness and a strong stand. They go hand and glove, together!

Yes, "my crowd" is a bit loud at times, but praise God, we are still standing for right and against wrong! Amen! "That's My Crowd!"

XXI. The Unspeakable Joy Crowd!
(I Cor. 2:14–16; 15:57–58; II Cor. 1:3–6, 20; 4:16)

A strong stand and a sweet spirit! It's the Bible way! Stand up, speak out, stay true, skin the skunks, but don't lose your spirit; don't do it with acid on your tongue. Do it in the love and compassion of Christ.

"Gloom! Despair! Agony, oh me!" That's the theme song of a lot of Christians! It's disgusting! "Rejoice...and again I say, Rejoice" (Phil. 4:4). That's the right spirit for a servant of God! "In every thing give thanks: for this is the will of God in Christ Jesus concerning you" (I Thess. 5:18). Whatever troubles you have, keep a heart of gratitude to God!

Circumstances and conditions! Troublesome times! Hurt and heartache! Disappointment and devastation! Betrayal! You name it—it's everywhere! If you don't have some of it right now, hang on, don't get the big head, take a deep breath and wait—your time is coming!

But don't sour! Don't vegetate spiritually! Don't get mouthy! Don't be a grump! Don't wear your feelings on your sleeve!

Reach up, get hold of God and live your faith triumphantly in the midst of the mudhole where you are mired!

Let no devil distract you! Let no cheap imitator of reality steal from you your spiritual birthright! A dozen times a day, light the fire in your heart from the glowing embers of God's altar!

When you consider who you are (a child of God); what you have (forgiveness, salvation, justification, redemption, regeneration, atonement, propitiation, the new birth and eternal security); and where you are going (Heaven), how on earth can you not have joy in your soul! Amen! "That's My Crowd!"

Conclusion...

What a crowd! Just think of the ones with whom you ought to be connected! I believe the crowd I've described here is the one you and I should run with—namely:

(1) The Unchangeable God Crowd, (2) The Unmistakable Jesus Crowd, (3) The Unedited Bible Crowd, (4) The Unrevokable Salvation Crowd, (5) The Unforgettable Heritage Crowd, (6) The Unalterable Fundamental Crowd, (7) The Unambiguous Doctrine Crowd, (8) The Unashamedly Local Church Crowd, (9) The Undisputably Separatist Crowd, (10) The Untiring Soul-Winning Crowd, (11) The Unintimidated Preaching Crowd, (12) The Uncompromising Music Crowd, (13) The Unwavering Standards Crowd, (14) The Undaunted Vision Crowd, (15) The Unceasing Prayer Crowd, (16) The Unrelenting Revival Crowd, (17) The

Unshakable Family Crowd, (18) The Unimpeachable Integrity Crowd, (19) The Unapologetically Premillennial Crowd, (20) The Unmovable Stand Crowd, (21) The Unspeakable Joy Crowd.

Amen! Amen! Amen! "That's My Crowd!"

Chapter 4

Taking a Stand

"Put on the whole armour of God, that ye may be able to stand against the wiles of the devil."

"Wherefore take unto you the whole armour of God, that ye may be able to withstand in the evil day, and having done all, to stand."—Eph. 6:11, 13.

Almost everyone agrees that Christians should take a stand! If not in fact, at least lip service is given to the premise! Independent, fundamental Baptists have a long heritage of standing and 'crying aloud.' It has been in the fabric of our heritage. We believe the necessity to take a stand is a major part of our scriptural mandate.

It is much easier, however, to stay seated, keep quiet and let things happen as they will! The popular thing in religious circles, even Christian circles, and now appearing often in independent Baptist circles as well, is (1) give in, (2) get together and (3) get along!

We believe, however, that such acquiescence, accommodation and appeasement are scripturally unacceptable, spiritually irresponsible and ethically reprehensible.

"Let's don't be so negative" is a favorite penchant of the voices of compromise! Notice, please, that they must be negative to get their message across that they don't want us to be negative! Oh, well!

Folks, you will rarely meet someone who is any more upbeat, excited and positive than I am. It's my mind-set! It's my lifestyle! But that doesn't mean I'm going to smile and agree to every proposal that's drawn out of the hat. Not at all!

Let me state very positively—I'm negative about some things! I'm negative about evolution! I'm negative about liquor! I'm negative about liberals! I'm negative about abortion! I'm negative about compromise! So far, so good? There's more!

I'm negative about using bad Bibles! I'm negative about contemporary-style music! I'm negative about ecumenism, even Baptist-flavored ecumenism! I'm negative about weak standards! I'm negative about running with the wrong crowd! I'm negative about promoting in our pulpits even good people who run with a bad crowd!

I'm positive about fundamentalism! I'm negative about mainstream evangelicalism!

I'm positive about Bible doctrine! I'm negative about ignoring it, eliminating it, adapting it or changing it!

I'm positive about the independent Baptist movement! I'm negative about the American Baptist Convention, the Southern Baptist Convention and other such groups!

I'm positive about pastor-led local churches! I'm negative about board-run, committee-bound, bureaucracy-laden church administration!

I'm positive about soul winning! I'm negative about lifestyle evangelism and whatever else replaces soul winning!

I'm positive about unity based on truth! I'm negative about peace at any price!

I'm positive about mounting an assault on the strongholds of Hell! I'm negative about the soft-spoken, feel-good agenda that "sees no evil, hears no evil," etc.

I'm positive the trend to "contemporize" is a bent toward compromise! I'm negative about even thinking of such!

I'm positive that "contemporary" in Christian circles means taking directions from the current crazes of the culture! I'm negative about doing that!

I'm positive that the time is now for God's people to take a stand. I'm negative about delaying it!

I'm positive taking a stand should start in the pulpit! I'm negative whenever and wherever that doesn't happen!

So, I'm positive about a lot of things, but I'm also absolutely, unequivocably negative about some others. Indeed, it seems inexplicable to me when we are positive about negative things or negative about positive things. Sometimes we are positive; at other times we are negative—and rightly so!

We caricature the wily politician who is mealymouthed, vacillating and waffling! The guy who changes his campaign promises from one town to the next is soon found out. He's the guy who goes with the money and the crowd. It is a sickening sight, but unfortunately quite common!

And then along comes a preacher, and God forbid that he should become an ambassador in the bonds of expediency! From his quiet corner of compromise, his stature is so lessened that even from tiptoe his voice is now a mere whisper. Where once a man of God stood tall with the thunder of a holy mandate, there is nothing but the faint echo of a hapless wimp!

"Wherefore he saith, Awake thou that sleepest, and arise from the dead, and Christ shall give thee light."—Eph. 5:14.

"Beloved, when I gave all diligence to write unto you of the common salvation, it was needful for me to write unto you, and exhort you that ye should earnestly contend for the faith which was once delivered unto the saints."—Jude 3.

Is the Message Enough?

A good bit is being said these days to try to convince us all that if the message is clear or if the doctrine is correct, then nothing else really matters.

It is the very mentality that has held sway with evangelicals for decades. It is unfortunately now the position taken by some independent Baptist groups.

But it is our strong feeling that the full picture is more than just the message. It is our conviction that methods matter! Motive matters! Money matters! Morals matter! Men matter! Ministry matters! Mission matters! There is in fact much that matters in addition to "just the message."

Some say as long as the Gospel is preached, they are willing to let other biblical matters go unaddressed. We believe that's shortsighted, ill advised and scripturally inadequate.

Others say as long as there is a body of doctrine on which we agree, nothing else matters. They say methods don't matter. They say associations don't matter.

It is this watered-down philosophy that is the basis on which some independent Baptist brethren now take their churches to ecumenical crusades (Graham, Palau, etc.); participate in Promise Keepers; adopt the "purpose-driven" philosophy; take up the contemporary church approach; use the charismatic style, praise and worship, including rock music; and go join the Southern Baptist Convention. This very same verbiage has been employed for generations by the proponents of every new compromise that's come along. "As long as I can preach the Gospel," they say, "nothing else matters." It is a formula for disaster!

The message is paramount! Obviously, if you don't have your message right, nothing else will matter. But it doesn't take much of an analysis of the past to discover that if some attention is NOT paid to method and motive, etc., and if there be no standard in these areas, then soon the message too is watered down, weakened and wasted.

So, we make no apology for raising these issues with our brethren.

Is the Method Really an Issue?

Yes, we think it is! Let me be specific:

(1) Some think the method of baptism is unimportant! We believe the Bible message is clear—believers should be baptized! We also believe the Bible method of baptism is immersion! Despite the fact that not everyone agrees, we believe the method does matter.

(2) Some think the method of Scripture doesn't matter! They want to take a Greek text that had 9,970 changes made in it in the 1880s and translate it so the Bible can be understood. Why would you want to understand a text that has been noticeably tampered with? Why tinker with it at all? What in the world has made it necessary in the past fifty years for us to roll out a new Bible every few months? It is nonsense to think that such can be done without eroding the people's confidence in the text.

(3) Some think the method of music doesn't matter! Their call for us to be "contemporary" is a clever way of saying, "We like what the culture is doing, and we want it at church."

So here they come—blaring, rocking and jiving! The Saturday night sounds of the nightclub down the street are front and center at the church house Sunday morning! It's only the start of a metamorphosis of ministry! Along with the rock 'n' roll music, the man of God will soon evolve into a cool dude, "Just As I Am" will be interpreted "Stay as you are," and the whims and fancies of the unsaved and the carnal will become the focus that compels us! It seems to me that the method of music ought to matter!

(4) Some think the method of associations doesn't matter! They are saying as long as you give a nod to our doctrinal statement, you may run with whomever you please and still be welcome in our fellowship. So ecclesiastical separation is out the door! For now they're just wanting to run with the Convention crowd. But they'll discover that the Convention crowd runs with a lot of others. It only takes a little buddy-buddy time with the Convention until it starts making sense to stretch your buddy circle to where the Convention has already gone. We are not at all happy with such reasoning.

We believe our fundamental platforms should showcase the people whose philosophy and practices are scripturally sound and worthy to be replicated. Associations do matter! Consider the unwise logic of saying, "Run with whomever you please." What parents would be wise to advise their children thusly? In like fashion, pastors and churches should give heed to their associations.

(5) Some think the "methodology" of ministry doesn't matter! Well, what happens then when the 8:30 a.m. service is truly (not just a joke) made into a mass? What if the Quaker practice of sitting silently and saying nothing at all were used? What if the pastoral staff has two lady "pastors"? What about the church that's sponsoring dances on the church property now?

Should the leader (pastor) of an independent Baptist church who goes this route be featured as a speaker at the next big national meeting? I don't think so! It seems to me that the *method* does matter!

Is the Motive an Issue?

Some would have us believe that as long as we get the job done, it doesn't matter *why* we do it. Admittedly, all of us have gotten the job done even at times when our motive was lacking. But the question here is whether or not motive is ever an issue. I believe it is! If you catch yourself improperly motivated, you ought to thump your own ear and kick your own shins until you get scripturally, rightly motivated!

It's never right to do wrong so we will have a chance to do a good thing!

So Let's Stand!

So, my brethren and my sisters, dear servants of Christ, sons and daughters of the Most High God, let's get a grip on what's taking place!

Let's not get enamored with the culture and whatever craze it's pushing at the moment!

Let's not forget that "contemporary" is rooted in the culture!

Let's remember that while the temptation is to be "cool," Hell is still hot!

Let's not give in to the casual approach when there is so much of major consequence, eternal matters that should require our best!

Let's not be ashamed to be fundamental!

Let's not flinch at being separatists!

Let's not repudiate the standards that are becoming to the servants of God!

Let's not swap soul winning for events, lifestyle, assimilation techniques, etc.

Let's keep a decent style of music at the church house!

Let's not toss the Bible overboard for some new watered-down, ink-is-still-wet version.

Let's not defrock the preacher and replace him with whatever else is available.

Let's not turn our churches over to committees to run!

Let's not bend amidst the prevailing winds of change. To do this so readily translates into compromise.

Let's keep the flag of Faith and faithfulness untarnished! Let's keep the banner stretched full and high!

Let's not dip our colors into compromise and carnality!

Let's be unapologetic and unafraid to "stand" and "having done all, to stand." Amen!

Chapter 5

In Times Like These

"For if thou altogether holdest thy peace at this time, then shall there enlargement and deliverance arise to the Jews from another place; but thou and thy father's house shall be destroyed: and who knoweth whether thou art come to the kingdom for such a time as this?"—Esther 4:14.

In a time when the well-being of the Jewish people was at stake and there was a fiendish plot concocted to destroy them, Mordecai challenged Queen Esther to use her influence and to utilize her position in an attempt to save her people. She had indeed come to the kingdom "for such a time as this."

I've always liked Ruth Caye Jones's song, "In Times Like These." It tells us that in times such as we face today we can feel like a ship being tossed on a rough sea. In that situation, the ship relies on its anchor for stability. There are some things that we need as anchors for our souls in the times in which we live. We need the Bible, and we need the Saviour who is revealed in it. Jesus is that Rock to which our anchor can hold, even in times like these.

We have a well-outlined description of our own times at several places in the Bible.

"As it is written, There is none righteous, no, not one:

"There is none that understandeth, there is none that seeketh after God.

"They are all gone out of the way, they are together become unprofitable; there is none that doeth good, no, not one.

"Their throat is an open sepulchre; with their tongues they have used deceit; the poison of asps is under their lips:

"Whose mouth is full of cursing and bitterness:

"Their feet are swift to shed blood:

"Destruction and misery are in their ways:

"And the way of peace have they not known:

"There is no fear of God before their eyes."—Rom. 3:10–18.

Consider also:

"Now the works of the flesh are manifest, which are these; Adultery, fornication, uncleanness, lasciviousness,

"Idolatry, witchcraft, hatred, variance, emulations, wrath, strife, seditions, heresies,

"Envyings, murders, drunkenness, revellings, and such like: of the which I tell you before, as I have also told you in time past, that they which do such things shall not inherit the kingdom of God."—Gal. 5:19–21.

And then there is the passage about "perilous times" which mirrors the newspaper on your desk today:

"This know also, that in the last days perilous times shall come.

"For men shall be lovers of their own selves, covetous, boasters, proud, blasphemers, disobedient to parents, unthankful, unholy,

"Without natural affection, trucebreakers, false accusers, incontinent, fierce, despisers of those that are good,

"Traitors, heady, highminded, lovers of pleasures more than lovers of God;

"Having a form of godliness, but denying the power thereof: from such turn away.

"For of this sort are they which creep into houses, and lead captive silly women laden with sins, led away with divers lusts,

"Ever learning, and never able to come to the knowledge of the truth."—II Tim. 3:1–7.

Now look at the recent happenings which give the face of reality to these scriptural predictions:

(1) The United States Supreme Court continues to misfire on key issues, as it did in the *Engel v. Vitale* case on prayer in public schools and the Madalyn Murray O'Hair case on Bible reading (1962 and 1963), as it did in *Roe v. Wade* in 1973, and now as in the Texas case on homosexuality in June 2003.

(2) The Roman Catholic Church, which has ensnared multiplied millions into a false religious system, has now been publicly exposed with widespread corruption with the homosexual pedophiles in the priesthood and the attempts of the hierarchy to cover it up.

(3) The Episcopalians in this country have a brewing scandal over their recent appointment of an openly avowed homosexual as bishop.

(4) Numerous other denominations, including Baptist, Methodist, Presbyterian, etc., have gone liberal theologically; and of course it soon begins to show in their polity and practice.

(5) Other groups like the Pentecostals and charismatics have had significant doctrinal problems all along, but with every passing day the stories that surface among them are increasingly ridiculous. Their major emphasis on miracles, healing, etc., necessitates one "evidence" and then another to support their claims. Much of it is manipulated and totally phony—in other words, an outright scam.

(6) "Contemporary" has become the word of choice in many modern churches. Think of the implications of the word: it has the scent and the flavor of the culture all over it.

(7) "These days" even some of our independent Baptist brethren are "contemporizing" and "ecumenicizing." For them, it is no longer legitimate to be separatist. They say they are trying to "find the center." Apparently that means developing relationships with groups who are not separatist, but ecumenical. So they start, inch by inch, one step at a time, to change. They feature speakers on their platforms from the SBC or other groups. Their music changes. Their program changes.

"In times such as these" are, it would be well for us to be sure we have our anchors down.

"Thou shalt not remove thy neighbour's landmark, which they of old time have set."—Deut. 19:14.

"Cursed be he that removeth his neighbour's landmark. And all the people shall say, Amen."—Deut. 27:17.

"Remove not the ancient landmark, which thy fathers have set."—Prov. 22:28.

"If the foundations be destroyed, what can the righteous do?"—Ps. 11:3.

"It was needful for me to write unto you, and exhort you that ye should earnestly contend for the faith which was once delivered unto the saints."—Jude 3.

"In times like these" we need

I. Men of God!

Preachers, pastors, missionaries and evangelists should be men of God—not crowd pleasers, not "cool dudes," not everybody's fishing buddies! They need to be men of God!

When the preacher walks into Wal-Mart, he needs to carry himself gracefully and graciously. When he visits the hospital, he should come prayerfully and compassionately. When he must go to the funeral home and the cemetery, he should minister comfort. When he visits a neighborhood, he must do so warmly and lovingly, yet urgently.

When he stands at the church house door, he is a shepherd and a prophet. When he strides to the pulpit, he does so with an open Bible to render the truth in terms even the children understand. He speaks not for himself but as the evangel of Christ, the vessel of the Holy Spirit and the ambassador of God.

Yes, indeed, "in times like these" we need the servants of faith to be men of God.

II. Great Churches!

"And they continued stedfastly in the apostles' doctrine and fellowship, and in breaking of bread, and in prayers."—Acts 2:42.

"Unto him be glory in the church by Christ Jesus throughout all ages, world without end. Amen."—Eph. 3:21.

From the first church on the planet (Jerusalem) to the church in your neighborhood, the Lord has a plan that is centered upon these local assemblies. It was never His plan that any church conform to the culture in which it was located. To the contrary, it is the divine plan that churches confront the culture with their message of salvation, morality, decency, order, and such like.

No church should let the times dictate its course; instead, every church should come to its task with a commitment to give the message of God clearly and convincingly.

The events and circumstances of today's headlines are quite real and cannot be ignored, but "these times" are not the proper gauge of what the church is or the catalyst to determine its message, its method, its manner or its ministry!

God intended that His church would be aggressive (Matt. 16:18). "The times" must not be our theme! "The times" must not be our thrust! "The times" are off center and off course! It is our assignment to tackle the times with the truth of God. We need men of God to lead the churches boldly and fearlessly to call the culture to repentance, regeneration and righteousness.

In every city, every town and in every country place where a church exists, may the breath of God enliven it and inflame it. May our churches take their places on the front lines of today's battles and do God's bidding "in times like these."

III. Soul Winners!

"In times like these" every Christian that has a heart to do the bidding of God should shed every vestige of carnality, let the Spirit of God give His power, and devote every energy to the reaching of unsaved sinners.

"They were all filled with the Holy Ghost, and they spake the word of God with boldness."—Acts 4:31.

"And daily in the temple, and in every house, they ceased not to teach and preach Jesus Christ."—Acts 5:42.

Soup lines, crisis shelters and clothes closets are wonderful things, but they are mere Band-Aids in comparison to the major surgery every sinner needs. So many of our churches are playing church, chasing themselves around the religious merry-go-round, talking big and doing virtually nothing!

"Awake to righteousness, and sin not; for some have not the knowledge of God: I speak this to your shame."—I Cor. 15:34.

That's right, there are people in your "Jerusalem" who are lost, and they have not been given the Gospel—not even one time. It is a "shame" (according to this text) for such to be the case.

Just think what would happen in America alone if 25,000 churches would avow themselves doctrinally fundamental, align themselves in uncompromising relationships and arrange their schedules to go after their cities! If we would train tens of thousands of fundamental, Bible-believing Christians to win souls and then give ourselves to the task, it would change the heart and the face of this nation. Oh, that it may be so "in these times"! Amen!

IV. Genuine Christians!

"In times like these" we surely do need some folks who will step up to the plate with a genuineness that shows plainly in every fiber of their being.

"Till I come, give attendance to reading, to exhortation, to doctrine.

"Neglect not the gift that is in thee."—I Tim. 4:13–14.

"And this I pray, that your love may abound yet more and more in knowledge and in all judgment;

"That ye may approve things that are excellent; that ye may be sincere and without offence till the day of Christ;

"Being filled with the fruits of righteousness, which are by Jesus Christ, unto the glory and praise of God."—Phil. 1:9–11.

The "hang-loose, anything-goes, no-standards" mentality that has invaded the church scene nationwide is not the biblical formula for success. If the demeanor and the deportment of Christians are so closely akin to the culture that you can't tell us from them, then the culture's floodtide is going to overwhelm us. There must be a distinguishable difference! There must be visible evidence of Christ in us, or the unsaved world will turn a deaf ear to our appeals.

I'm not suggesting that the unseparated folks are not saved. They may be—in fact, they are, if they have trusted Christ (Eph. 2:8–10). What I am saying is that "in these times," if you expect to make an impact for Christ, you'd better shape up your act. "Genuine" runs down to the depths of your soul, and it also emerges on the surface where it can be seen. The more *real* you are inside, the more evidence there will likely be outside. When you are copying the hippies, mimicking Hollywood and enthralled with the drug scene, you are at best immature and ill advised. As maturity begins to get a footing in your Christian experience, you are going to find motivation to follow Christ—and Paul, John R. Rice, Charles Haddon Spurgeon, D. L. Moody and others whose example is worthy of a Christian testimony.

"In these times" we just need some sons and daughters of God who will "walk worthy" (Eph. 4:1) and demonstrate with clear voice that they are *genuine!* Amen!

V. Strong Families!

From the creation to this very moment it has been a part of God's plan that we have families.

"So God created man in his own image, in the image of God created he him; male and female created he them.

"And God blessed them, and God said unto them, Be fruitful, and multiply, and replenish the earth."—Gen. 1:27–28.

"Lo, children are an heritage of the LORD: and the fruit of the womb is his reward.

"As arrows are in the hand of a mighty man; so are children of the youth.

"Happy is the man that hath his quiver full of them."—Ps. 127:3–5.

It is not enough for a man and a woman simply to live out their days together. *Family* means much more than mere convenience or accommodation. It means love, support, encouragement, nurture, protection and happiness together.

A husband and wife must yield themselves to God (Eph. 5:21) and then to each other (Eph. 5:22–31). It is the cornerstone of our society.

When children arrive at your house, they should not be given leadership roles. They are not the CEOs of your family. You are to lead and teach, love and train them. They are supposed to follow you as you lead.

Television and the Internet are not family-friendly. If you do not severely restrict access to and usage of both, they will totally undermine your best intentions. They will effectively steal your children from you. You cannot allow kids unlimited exposure to values and ideas totally foreign to what you believe, without paying a dear price.

You must spend time with your family. Do chores together, talk about almost everything, eat together regularly, play together, pray and read the Bible together, and be full participants at your church.

Be very careful about where they go to school, including college.

Dad must take the lead and be husband and daddy enthusiastically.

Mom must give herself to being wife and mother enthusiastically.

Discipline must not be left to chance! Do it! Undisciplined children are NOT happy kids—and neither is anyone close to them happy.

"In these times" strong families are a vital part of the need in our nation. Christians especially must not fail in this arena.

VI. Christian Education!

In the early years of our nation, all education was Christian education. Then we entered into a period where the government took charge of education but included Christian values and concepts. But in Stage 3 of our educational history, the "progressive education" advocates began a purge designed to erase all things Christian from the public arena. Subtle at first and cleverly cloaked in patriotic terms, the efforts intensified in the 1960s. In the forty years that followed, the liberals took off the gloves and began to fight in bold and brazen fashion. Their goal, which has been by and large achieved, has been to (1) eradicate every vestige of our Judeo-Christian heritage from every classroom, kindergarten to graduate school; (2) and to institute a secularistic, humanistic, atheistic philosophy in the entire educational arena. Furthermore, the new system has been permitted to speak and to act in hostile fashion to Christian philosophy and toward anyone who chooses to be openly Christian while in the educational system.

"In times like these" our churches have had to become pro-active again in education. It is, we believe, absolutely essential that Christian families protect their children from the government-controlled educational system now in place.

Furthermore, Christian families need to select carefully the places where they send their youngsters to college. Higher education can have a very high price tag attached to it that has much greater consequences than the dollar figures.

We recommend that every family place their college-aged young people in very clear-cut fundamental Bible colleges. If they want to train for some professional field, then there are also Christian schools where they can go.

Remember, you are responsible for assisting and leading your child. Though a school may have a great academic reputation or whatever else, be sure you don't toss your student into a den of philosophic rattlesnakes (or worse).

Christian education is a vital necessity "in these times."

VII. Publishing!

"In these times" the publishing world, along with the other media outlets (radio, TV, the Internet), is churning out garbage twenty-four hours a day, seven days a week. Even in religious circles, the books, the tapes and the programs are filled with half-truths and outright falsehoods. Heresy is enjoying a heyday.

Christian psychology and other Milquetoast matters have become the standard fare. "Soft and easy" is the demand. What a sad state of affairs!

So here we are! For seventy years the Sword of the Lord Publishers has, in our newspaper and in our books, tapes, etc., taken a strong, biblical, moral stand. We have been unashamedly and fearlessly giving voice to the issues and causes that honor the Lord. Everywhere I go someone says to me, "The voice of the Sword is needed and necessary—now more than ever." I agree.

Thousands of churches should be getting dozens, if not hundreds, of copies of each SWORD issue and with deliberate effort getting them out to their people and into their communities.

Just imagine, if we could distribute 5,000 to 10,000 copies of each issue of the SWORD OF THE LORD in each of the fifty states, the impact it would have on this nation! We pray that more and more folks will get the vision and get it out in their areas. We do a lot already, but we need to multiply our efforts many times over "for such a time as this." Amen!

Conclusion

There is no question that a lot of things are in a mess across the land, but you and I must avoid a "nothing can be done" attitude. We just need to get on our knees often and then stand on our feet to make our presence felt.

Every pulpit needs a straightforward, solid, steady, seasoned, scriptural voice that will "cry aloud" and "spare not" (Isa. 58:1). For "such a time" nothing less will do!

Is there not a Queen Esther in our midst? What about a Moses? a Joseph? perhaps a Daniel? or an Isaiah or a Jeremiah? Could we not find an Elijah here and there, an Elisha too? Are there not some John the Baptist types, some Stephens and Philips, and some Paul and Silas preachers?

Oh, dear God, "in times like these" let it be so! Amen!

Chapter 6
"Contend for the Faith"

"Beloved, when I gave all diligence to write unto you of the common salvation, it was needful for me to write unto you, and exhort you that ye should earnestly contend for the faith which was once delivered unto the saints."—Jude 3.

Look carefully at the words "...earnestly contend...." They are pointed and when they are understood they are powerful.

"Contend" can be a matter of struggle. It is a competition against an opponent. There is a contrast, a matter of great concern and great reason about which we must be willing to be a combtant. Half-heart energy is not worthy of this conflict! It is a cause to which we must attend earnestly!

"...For the faith...." Not our preferences, but the Faith! Not some private agenda, but the Faith! Not some popular pasttime but the Faith!

"Is there not a cause?" (I Sam. 17:29). "Is there not a cause" for us? "Is there not a cause" today? There is! There is!

You ask, "Why should I get into the battle?" In verse 4 we learn the details.

I. "Contend for the Faith" Because of the Disputers

"For there are certain men crept in unawares, who were before of old ordained to this condemnation, ungodly men, turning the grace of our God into lasciviousness, and denying the only Lord God, and our Lord Jesus Christ."

There are those who dispute the claims of Christ; they dispute

49

the position of God. They do not come in and say openly and honestly, "I am a jerk" or "I am a creep" or "I am a liberal" or "I am an apostate." Instead, they sneak upon you. They creep in inch by inch with their ungodly agenda, even in some cases denying the Lord God Himself! Often smiling and patting you on the back, giving lip service to the ministry of God, they are all the while getting in position to dispute the truth. They dispute Creation. They dispute the crossing of the Red Sea. They dispute the destruction of the walls of Jericho. They go ballistic over Jonah. They dispute the virgin birth. They reduce the resurrection to mere resuscitation. They dispute salvation without works. They like form and ceremony, but they dispute the power of God.

These are the disputers who disparage the reality of God and whose voices, like a wrecking ball, destroy the good, the godly, the beautiful and the eternal. Beware the disputers, and "contend for the faith" against their antics!

II. "Contend for the Faith" Because of Disbelievers

"I will therefore put you in remembrance, though ye once knew this, how that the Lord, having saved the people out of the land of Egypt, afterward destroyed them that believed not."—Vs. 5.

It is staggering when you consider how we choose to forget the things that we once knew. It is amazing that there is such wholesale changing of the substance and the style of things. At one time we had standards, and we had a clear-cut identity, but now so many among us want to be just like the worldly folks down the street.

Jude points out that there are people who once walked with God, but they bought into faithlessness; they have deliberately chosen not to walk with God by faith. Instead they are saying, "Well, we don't know whether or not God is really going to help us. We don't actually know for sure that we ought to be following Moses out to the Red Sea." Once they got there, they said, "We've taken a wrong turn. What kind of a road map did Moses use? Who gave him directions that got us here?"

You say, "What was the matter with them when they were mouthing and murmuring like that?" It was unbelief!

We read the Bible, but then we say, "We'd better get a committee

50

together and talk over this matter." The plain instructions of the Bible are unmistakable, yet we want to get five or six people together who don't know whether or not they even believe the Bible. If they did, they would just say, "Hey, we don't have to caucus on this. God has already spoken!"

Instead the standard procedure is to put a committee together who will then vote 3-2 on whether or not to do the will of God. That absolutely reeks with the stench of carnality upon it! You say, "Don't talk about our committees like that." If you get a committee together to talk about what God has already spoken, it *is* a "stinking" committee.

You ask, "What's the problem?" We're talking about being just like the Israelites who were dragging their feet, who did not believe God, who had every indication that they had the presence of God, but they just wouldn't follow Him.

He said, "You'd better pay attention, because not following God doesn't pay." You never do yourself good when you start doubting God!

When you say, "I don't know whether or not God is God; I don't know whether I ought to follow Him; I don't know if He really means business," you will never get in where God wants to lead you.

III. "Contend for the Faith" Because of the Disloyal

*"And the angels which kept not their first estate, but left their own habitation, he hath reserved in everlasting chains under darkness unto the judgment of the great day."—*Vs. 6.

The point of disloyalty is a matter of faith. These angels had position, they were close to God, but they turned on Him. They said, "We're just not going to pay attention to God anymore. We'd rather do something our own way! We'd rather do things the way we want to do them than to do them God's way!"

There ought to be a sense of loyalty to God. Carl Sagan knows the truth now (he's dead), but he used to get on television and try to convince us that there was no God, that there was no creation, that we evolved up out of the primordial ooze somewhere.

When someone says things like that, he invariably makes it sound so plausible and so interesting. You'd better remember that there is a God in Heaven and pay no attention to Dr. Johnny-Come-Lately with his Ph.D. hanging off his ears. You just say, "There is a God in Heaven who knows more than the university knows, so I'll just stick with Him!" Otherwise, you have disloyalty like these disloyal angels.

IV. "Contend for the Faith" Because of the Degenerates

"Even as Sodom and Gomorrha, and the cities about them in like manner, giving themselves over to fornication, and going after strange flesh, are set forth for an example, suffering the vengeance of eternal fire."—Vs. 7.

We're talking about people fornicating and chasing after flesh. We're talking about people adulterating themselves. We're talking about people taking their sexual purity and throwing it away. In effect, they are prostituting something that God says is good and right and pure, and making it wrong and bad for themselves.

"Even as Sodom and Gomorrha...going after strange flesh" is a hint toward homosexuality. Sodom was the main capital, the headquarters, the West Hollywood of the ancient world.

He is saying that these pocket centers where the queers have gathered in such great numbers had better pay attention because there is an eternal fire of vengeance that comes when people turn away from God and go their own directions.

It makes me sick that Hollywood laughs about homosexuality. They put these silly sitcoms together to teach our society, including our children, to play loose with everything and to run with everyone and anyone. It is a degeneracy that erodes the very foundation of our society.

V. "Contend for the Faith" Because of the Defilers

"Likewise also these filthy dreamers defile the flesh, despise dominion, and speak evil of dignities."—Vs. 8.

Just like Jude spoke of the disputers in verse 4, the disbelievers in verse 5, the disloyal in verse 6, the degenerates in verse 7, here in verse 8 he talks about the defilers. God says, "Pay attention! An awful vengeance comes for that level of defilement."

Mark it down: that is exactly what this crowd does. They "despise dominion," meaning they despise authority. They don't care that there is a Bible, that there is a God. So when some preacher stands up and talks against homosexuality, they say, "Hey, that's a hate speech! Someone is liable to hear you condemning the homosexual lifestyle, get all enflamed, then go out and do something bad to a homosexual."

Let me tell you this: the fact that we stand against bank robbers doesn't mean we are guilty of hate speech against bank robbers! This whole homosexual crowd has a group in Washington eating out of their hands. These amoral and spineless politicians are bowing to and saluting them at every turn in the road.

I look forward to somebody's standing up one of these days and saying, "I am running for office, and I believe in the monogamous family relationship that God set up in the Book of Genesis!"

It would be wonderful if some politician had enough backbone to stand up and say, "We were better off when the 'filthy dreamers' were in the closet somewhere!"

America has gone downhill since these defilers got out on Main Street.

You say, "What's the problem here?" They despise authority, defile the flesh and speak evil of dignities (things that are good).

If they keep going with this thing on hate speech, they will soon have it to the place that when a preacher preaches strongly like this, the police will be called in. He will pay a fine or spend time in jail simply because he was preaching biblical truth! We are close to that now!

VI. "Contend for the Faith" Because of the Defamers

"Yet Michael the archangel, when contending with the devil he disputed about the body of Moses, durst not bring against him a railing accusation, but said, The Lord rebuke thee."—Vs. 9.

This verse is talking about defamation. These characters not only get low-down, but they lambaste good people. They talk evil of godly things. They speak against all that is right and good.

VII. "Contend for the Faith" Because of Devils

We have degenerates, defilers, defamers and now, absolute devils.

"But these speak evil of those things which they know not: but what they

know naturally, as brute beasts, in those things they corrupt themselves.

"Woe unto them! for they have gone in the way of Cain, and ran greedily after the error of Balaam for reward, and perished in the gainsaying of Core.

"These are spots in your feasts of charity, when they feast with you, feeding themselves without fear: clouds they are without water, carried about of winds; trees whose fruit withereth, without fruit, twice dead, plucked up by the roots;

"Raging waves of the sea, foaming out their own shame; wandering stars, to whom is reserved the blackness of darkness for ever.

"And Enoch also, the seventh from Adam, prophesied of these, saying, Behold, the Lord cometh with ten thousands of his saints,

"To execute judgment upon all, and to convince all that are ungodly among them of all their ungodly deeds which they have ungodly committed, and of all their hard speeches which ungodly sinners have spoken against him.

"These are murmurers, complainers, walking after their own lusts; and their mouth speaketh great swelling words, having men's persons in admiration because of advantage.

"But, beloved, remember ye the words which were spoken before of the apostles of our Lord Jesus Christ;

"How that they told you there should be mockers in the last time, who should walk after their own ungodly lusts.

"These be they who separate themselves, sensual, having not the Spirit."—Vss. 10–19.

America Has Set Herself Against God!

The word "beloved" is used three times (verses 3, 17 and 20) in the Book of Jude. I think it makes an absolutely good division, a natural outline, for the book.

He is saying in verse 17, "Beloved, in the midst of all this darkness, in the midst of all of these defilers and defamers and degenerates who are operating and working, remember the words which were spoken by the apostles. Don't forget the guidelines! Don't forget the values of the kingdom! Remember the words which were spoken by the apostles."

I believe what we've read here is strangely akin to a biography of America.

Seven words show us the way to self-destruction:

Contempt!

The 21st century days in which we live are ones of absolute contempt for God. He could charge us with contempt of court, and it would be a valid charge!

America has set herself against God. Mrs. Madalyn O'Hair decided that she wanted to purge the public school system of prayer and Bible reading. In 1962 and again in 1963 an absolutely silly Supreme Court agreed with her. And now, we have people all over America—led by the lawyers of the ACLU—jumping up and down applauding. In my book, anything that crowd applauds deserves to be looked at more closely and with suspicion!

As a rule of thumb, if I want to find out whether something is right or wrong, I find out where the ACLU stands, then I stand on the other side.

This contempt for God has taken root in America. The hippies came on the scene, preaching contempt: "Don't tell us what to do! You are an absolute legalist if you try to give us any rules! We're going to run the show, do what we want to do, and we're not going to ask anybody."

Well, the hippies came and went, but their philosophy took hold in America. That contempt which they peddled in the 1960s is now the norm on Main Street, USA—absolute contempt!

There was a time when you had to go to a university somewhere to get anybody to articulate evolution or humanism. But now little kids in the third grade can spout the stuff and argue with you because they have been spoonfed those wicked philosophies over and over and over from almost the time of their birth in America!

Carnality!

We have a situation now where there is absolute contempt for God, and when contempt takes hold, carnality will be its buddy. Carnality will come, and the activities of the natural man and the carnalities of a Christian are all the same business. When the people of God adopt the disobedience of the world and take on the character and the ways of the world, we have a wave of carnality, and this wave of carnality will spread into the families, into the schools and into the churches.

I am a mild-mannered man, yet these days I have to be prepared when I get up and talk openly about things, because somebody is very likely to come up and charge into me. Twice in the last month I have had someone come up after a service and absolutely shellac me because of something I had said. I am just trying to beat the drum and call the shots like they ought to be called. I'm saying, "Good is good, and bad is bad." But nowadays people don't just disagree with you; they storm up to you and tell you off!

What's happening? Contempt has set in, and carnality has taken root. And whenever preachers determine to be like Elijah and Elisha and John the Baptist and other great men of God out of the Bible and call a skunk a skunk, brother, they'd better be prepared!

Compromise!

We have contempt, followed by carnality, then compromise comes.

You say, "That sounds like something the church is doing." You are right. You go into many of the churches now, and you never know from which Bible they will be preaching.

You ask, "Why is that such a big deal?" Some of the popular "Bibles" they are now printing don't have all of it there. They've taken out portions of it.

You say, "Oh, I guess they just happened to forget them." No, they did it on purpose. They found things that didn't suit them. They take words like "the blood" and change them to the "the death." You say that doesn't seem like all that big a deal. It *is* a big deal. The word *blood* is blood, and the word *death* is death.

The Bible doesn't say, "The life of the flesh is in the *death*." It says, "The life of the flesh is in the *blood* [emphasis added]" (Lev. 17:11). Even though a man may bleed to death, there is a difference between bleeding and dying.

When they start tampering with the Bible, there is always a reason and purpose behind it. I promise you that if you read these other Bibles, you are getting on a downhill slide.

This same crowd of compromisers want to use some softsoap Bible that doesn't cut to the heart. They say, "In our church, we just don't talk a lot about doctrine. You can just come in here and believe whatever you want to believe."

Doctrine is on the first and last pages of the Bible and on all the pages in between. If you dismiss doctrine, then you are denying the Bible.

"In the beginning God..."—that's doctrine. "In the beginning God created..."—that's doctrine.

Perhaps you ask, "Do we really need to make a big to-do about that? Can't you just make space for the evolutionists?" I'd be glad to teach doctrine to a church full of evolutionists, but they don't teach anything in my church! I'm sorry, sir, but the Bible says, "Neither give place to the devil" (Eph. 4:27). When a man lines up with evolution, he's in the same line as the devil. That deserves "no place" in God's work.

You may say, "We're going to let them run some of the kids' clubs and run bus routes." No! They need to get straight on the doctrine first! Doctrine is important, and if you let them have a position in your church, you too become a no-good compromiser. Call it secondary separation if you wish, but you are, in my judgment, a two-bit, tinhorn compromiser!

It starts with contempt for God; then carnality takes hold; after which they begin to say, "Hey, anything goes. Come on in. We really don't care what you believe."

The first thing you know, you're saying, "I think we would like to hire an associate pastor who is enough of a diplomat so that he can help us." So you hire an associate pastor who wears pinstripes to hide the yellow stripe down his back, and the next thing you know, the people want a preacher like that!

I can show you places all over America where some church has brought in a preacher who doesn't have a backbone to stand up and say "No!" with any authority. He is a mere puppet on a string taking orders from some board. He has no voice; he is only an echo. The average church today is a cesspool of such compromise. Everybody is just there, trying not to hurt one another's feelings: "Whoa! We don't want anybody to get upset!"

God help us! We're not doing much if we don't get somebody upset every once in a while.

Collaboration!

Then collaboration joins contempt, carnality and compromise to create the Unity Quartet.

These folks begin to collaborate with the compromising crowd and the cultic crowd and the charismatic crowd.

You say, "The TBN crowd is going to be at the civic center."

They're bringing their music, their heretical teachings, their pseudo-healing lines, their unbiblical babble and their blab-it-and-grab-it prosperity gospel. Rod Parsley and Benny Hinn will slay them by some spirit and throw them in every aisle! Maybe so! But we are not going to be there!

"But our choir wants to go and be on the platform and be a part of it."

No! No! No! We're just not going!

You ask, "What's wrong with Benny Hinn?" He's a heretic! Phony baloney!

How do I know all that? I've taken the time to study the charismatic movement. Their charades are absolutely phony. They are designed to manipulate the crowds psychologically and to fleece them monetarily. That's right! It's money, money, money—don't you forget it!

Their healing ministries are a sham as well! They went through a period of time where they were lengthening legs. They would set a man down and tell him that his back was hurting because one leg was shorter than the other. I can show you exactly how they did that; it was all in how they seated you in the chair. Within one second I can make your right leg shorter than the left, then reverse it by changing how I seat you in the chair. It's no miracle; it's monkey business! It's a dishonest manipulation of the naive and the vulnerable!

It is absolutely a scam and phony!

Let me thump another thing while I'm here! Does the name Anne Graham Lotz register with you? She's the preaching daughter of Billy Graham, the world's most famous ecumenical, compromising evangelist.

He used to be on the board of the Sword of the Lord. He got off in 1957. Why? Because he made a compromising turn (yes, in 1957!) in his ministry, and he said to Dr. John R. Rice, "You're not going to like the turn that I've made in my ministry, and I think maybe I ought to get off the Sword board."

That was almost fifty years ago.

Now he has a daughter, Anne Lotz. Graham himself says, and I quote, "She's the best preacher in the family."

Mrs. Lotz tours across America. She was in Knoxville recently, and she drew 25,000 in the stadium there.

You ask, "What on earth are they doing?" They are starting to sell the "women preachers" to America. What is wrong with that? Well, the last time I checked, the Bible did have something to say about it.

Confusion!

We're talking about collaborating with the compromisers and the cult crowd and the charismatic crowd. There is a logical step right after contempt and carnality and compromise and collaboration—and that is confusion.

You have people who come up to you and say, "We don't know what is real and what is not. We don't know whether we have the right Bible. We don't know which church is right."

Whence did all the confusion come? It started when we got contempt for God, plunged off into carnality, then started compromising and collaborating with the compromisers. Confusion is simply the harvest to be reaped for the seeds sown and cultivated.

Crisis!

We have crisis because people start saying, "Whatever I think is right is what I want to do. I'll do whatever I want to do, I don't care what the preacher says or what the Bible says." The first thing you know, their kids are saying, "We don't care what you say, Daddy! You don't care what the Bible says, and you don't care what the preacher says."

Or some little ten-year-old will look at his mother and say, "You can't tell me what to do!" After all, they have already given him a phone number at school so he can call social workers anytime you frown at him in a way that he doesn't want to be frowned at. You lay a finger on him and see how quickly he will use that phone number.

"Where did all that start?" you ask. When you decided you weren't going to walk with God and you weren't going to pay attention to the church or the Bible. You sowed seeds of destruction in your own kids.

Condemnation!

Oh, how the world hates the term and the thought of condemnation! The religionists of our day don't want us even to use the word because it so easily offends people. The condemned people (John 3:18) don't want to be told of the gravity of their situation. But hear me clearly! If you walk the way of contempt, carnality, compromise, collaboration, confusion, crisis, mark it down: condemnation is in the offing for you.

I'm talking about a path that will lead your kids straight to Hell! They will be condemned! It's a path that will take America to the graveyard.

How did we get to the place where we had a president like Bill Clinton who didn't know the meaning of the word *is?* Can you believe we had a president who answered a question under oath with, "It all depends on what you mean by 'is'"! You would think he might pick out some big, long word, but, oh no, he uses a two-letter word—*is.*

You say, "Well, he was trying to scam us." You're exactly right. He knew better. It was a bold-faced lie designed to deceive the people and protect his position. How could this be? How could it happen? I will tell you where it all started.

It did not start in the White House. It did not start with the politicians—they only picked up on it. When I was going to the theological "cemetery" in the 1960s, I sat in class after class after class where they asked, "Is the Bible the Word of God?" Or they would say perhaps the Word of God is there, if you and I can determine which word is God's and which is not!

They were saying, "The Bible *is not* really the Word of God; it only *contains* the Word of God." And we debated in those days the meaning of the word *is.* The politicians found out about it and said, "If you preachers don't know anything, if you don't have any absolutes, and if you don't stand for anything, then we don't have to stand for anything either!"

The reason we have corrupt politicians is that we have had an erosion of absoluteness at the church house, and condemnation comes because of it. The multitudes of our 21st-century world are like nomads in a philosophical wilderness, wandering around hungry and thirsty and not knowing where to stop to eat and drink.

"Remember Ye the Words… of the Apostles"

Verse 17 says, "Remember ye the words…of the apostles." Read them, receive them, report them.

In November of 1999 I had two back-to-back meetings in New England. I said to my wife, "If you'll go with me, we'll take a couple of days off at the end of the second meeting and tour some historical places."

We did the first meeting and then the second meeting. On Thursday morning we got a rental car and drove several hours to our first stop: Northfield, Massachusetts, the birthplace, home and burial place of Dwight L. Moody.

I stood in Moody's pulpit. That big auditorium was built in 1894 (five years before he died). The acoustics were wonderful. Even though it seats approximately two thousand people, there is no amplification, no public address system, but one can hear right up to the top of the balcony. In those days they knew how to build a building right.

It was a cold day in November, but we walked across to the burial site, which is also on the campus of Northfield School. I stood beside the place where Moody and his wife are buried. My wife took several pictures.

Moody

As I stood there, I thought about how God had so mightily used D. L. Moody. He was not a tutored man. He had not gone to college. Sometime after he got saved, he just started rounding up kids in Chicago. Soon he had something going. Then somebody invited him to speak here and there, and before long he was absolutely shaking America and Europe. Tens of thousands of people were saved through his ministry.

There was no debate in his mind as to whether or not the Bible was the Bible. There was no debate in his mind whether or not people were lost and dying. There was an urgency in his message and in his ministry!

Edwards

The next day we drove across the state line into Enfield, Connecticut. There in that tiny village is a little historical marker to mark the spot where on July 8, 1741, Jonathan Edwards preached his famous sermon, "Sinners in the Hands of an Angry God."

He was a great preacher, perhaps the most brilliant intellect of his day. He was the president of Princeton University (called the College of New Jersey in those days) when he died. He was so nearsighted, he had big, thick lenses in his glasses. He didn't get up and preach free-style; he wrote out his sermons, and with his face down close to the page he read them word for word.

God moved in that one particular meeting with this nearsighted preacher. What began that day in Enfield, Connecticut spread in village after village all across New England. Tens of thousands of people were saved in the months following that sermon.

Torrey

Once when I was in Wilkes-Barre, Pennsylvania, I said to the pastor, "If we could do so on Monday, I would like to go over to Montrose." Montrose is the home and the burial place of R. A. Torrey.

Dwight L. Moody had an understudy who worked with him for years. His name was Reuben Archer Torrey. Moody was the untutored man who had never been to school, while Torrey was the brilliant intellectual. When Moody died in 1899, Torrey picked up the mantle, and for the next twenty-nine years he too went across the country, beating the drum and crying aloud, "God is God! The Bible is the Bible! Men are lost! Heaven is real! Hell is hot!" God used Torrey mightily during those days.

As I stood by his burial site, I prayed, "O God, I pray that You will light that same fire in my heart as You did in the hearts of Torrey and Moody and Edwards. Help me to impact this world of darkness."

These men remembered the Word of God. They said that the Word of God is real! They did not try to invent new words or a new message or new concepts; they simply cried out what God had given to a nation that was lost and dying and condemned.

In the midst of the confusion and collaboration with the enemy, these giants of faith, holy men of God, spoke clearly the message of God. It is here in the Word of God that we find the will of God, the wisdom of God and the ways of God. It is a responsibility to "contend" for all of this "which was once delivered unto the saints" (Jude 3).

In a world of darkness, with a thousand clamoring voices that would lead you down the primrose path to the Devil's place, hear me: "Remember ye the words... of the apostles." Then raise your voice to make them heard! You are opposed! Contend! You are criticized! Contend! You are refused! Contend!

Chapter 7

Mixed Signals Confuse
Salvation Message

Life is short and death is sure. Then comes eternity. Eternity is forever—and it will be spent by every one of us in one of two places—Heaven or Hell.

Heaven, the great place where God Himself lives, where all of us would like to go after our death, is a wonderful, absolutely incredible paradise. Hell, on the other hand, is a house of horrors, a place so gross, so deplorable that no one in his right mind would choose to spend even a few minutes there, much less an eternity.

The Bible gives a clear picture of a real Heaven and a real Hell, actual places, literal to the most minute of details. Every living human being will spend eternity in one place or the other.

With a sin debt weighing so heavily upon us that Hell is sure to be our eternal lot and without even a wisp of hope that we could make Heaven, what could possibly be of greater importance to any of us than the subject of salvation? It is an absolutely crucial contemplation and one which simply must not get bungled up!

A Real Hell

"And it came to pass, that the beggar died, and was carried by the angels into Abraham's bosom: the rich man also died, and was buried;

"And in hell he lift up his eyes, being in torments, and seeth Abraham afar off, and Lazarus in his bosom.

"And he cried and said, Father Abraham, have mercy on me, and send Lazarus, that he may dip the tip of his finger in water, and cool my tongue; for I am tormented in this flame."

"And beside all this, between us and you there is a great gulf fixed: so

that they which would pass from hence to you cannot; neither can they pass to us, that would come from thence.

"Then he said, I pray thee therefore, father, that thou wouldest send him to my father's house:

"For I have five brethren; that he may testify unto them, lest they also come into this place of torment."—Luke 16:22–24, 26–28.

A Real Heaven

"And I saw no temple therein: for the Lord God Almighty and the Lamb are the temple of it.

"And the city had no need of the sun, neither of the moon, to shine in it: for the glory of God did lighten it, and the Lamb is the light thereof.

"And the nations of them which are saved shall walk in the light of it: and the kings of the earth do bring their glory and honour into it.

"And the gates of it shall not be shut at all by day: for there shall be no night there.

"And they shall bring the glory and honour of the nations into it.

"And there shall in no wise enter into it any thing that defileth, neither whatsoever worketh abomination, or maketh a lie: but they which are written in the Lamb's book of life."—Rev. 21:22–27.

With the reality of both Heaven and Hell in full focus, the question must be posed, and promptly so, How does a person escape Hell and have a secure residence in Heaven? Again we must look to the Bible for the answer.

Salvation a Must!

Just as the message on Heaven and Hell is clear, so the scriptural word on salvation is quite plain and discernibly clear.

"Neither is there salvation in any other: for there is none other name under heaven given among men, whereby we must be saved."—Acts 4:12.

"He that believeth on him is not condemned: but he that believeth not is condemned already, because he hath not believed in the name of the only begotten Son of God."—John 3:18.

"Verily, verily, I say unto thee, Except a man be born again, he cannot

see the kingdom of God."—John 3:3.

So salvation is the means of escaping Hell, and at the same time it is the necessary ticket for Heaven.

"For the Son of man is come to seek and to save that which was lost."— Luke 19:10.

"And it shall come to pass, that whosoever shall call on the name of the Lord shall be saved."—Acts 2:21.

"For whosoever shall call upon the name of the Lord shall be saved."— Rom. 10:13.

Salvation Is Available Only in Jesus Christ!

That's right! Only in Jesus Christ! Not in Buddha, not in humanitarian effort, not in an improved lifestyle, not by whom you know, not by color or creed or country, not by performance of good works—not any of that, not all of it combined! But rather, only in Christ.

"Neither is there salvation in any other: for there is none other name under heaven given among men, whereby we must be saved."— Acts 4:12.

Salvation in Christ provides everlasting life in Heaven for poor, sinful human beings such as you and I. We do not deserve it, cannot earn it and are incapable of attaining it except through Him.

"For by grace are ye saved through faith; and that not of yourselves: it is the gift of God:
"Not of works, lest any man should boast."—Eph. 2:8, 9.

"Jesus saith unto him, I am the way, the truth, and the life: no man cometh unto the Father, but by me."—John 14:6.

Now Comes the Confusion!

The message of salvation is being so garbled by so many religious spokespeople, it is no wonder that so many millions are baffled and bewildered by it all.

"For if the trumpet give an uncertain sound, who shall prepare himself to the battle?"—I Cor. 14:8.

Catholics Sending False Signals

The Roman Catholic pope recently (September 5, 2000) approved a Vatican document in which they claimed salvation was possible only through the Roman Catholic Church. Of course, the truth is that no church is the vehicle of salvation. Membership as a Catholic, a Baptist or whatever is worthless to secure salvation. You simply do not get saved that way. Church membership is not the remedy for getting sins forgiven, and it does not secure Heaven even for a moment—not for Catholics or Baptists or any other person.

> Tempering a controversial Vatican declaration on salvation, Pope John Paul II said Wednesday (December 6) that all who live a just life will be saved even if they do not believe in Jesus Christ and the Roman Catholic Church.
>
> ...[A]ddressing some 30,000 pilgrims gathered in St. Peter's Square....
>
> "The gospel teaches us that those who live in accordance with the Beatitudes—the poor in spirit, the pure of heart, those who bear lovingly the sufferings of life—will enter God's kingdom," John Paul said.
>
> "All who seek God with a sincere heart, including those who do not know Christ and His church, contribute under the influence of grace to the building of His kingdom," he said.
>
> The pope appeared to take a far more inclusive approach to salvation than the declaration "Dominus Iesus" issued September 5 by the Congregation for the Doctrine of the Faith, which serves as the Vatican's guardian of doctrinal orthodoxy.
>
> *—CHRISTIAN NEWS, 12/18/00*

Sadly, so many millions listen to this man, and since he is a religious leader with millions of followers, many of them hang breathlessly on his every utterance! Unfortunately, his voice is not that of a true man of God, and his pontifications obscure the true message of salvation in the process!

If he is right this time (December 6), that people can be saved by living the good life—and he says, "...even if they do not believe in

Jesus"—then obviously, the Roman Catholic document (September 5) entitled "Dominus Iesus" was not correct! The two statements are totally at odds with each other, so quite obviously at least one of them must be wrong! In fact, both of them are false, misleading misrepresentations of the true message of Christ!

We believe the Bible, God's Word, is the authoritative statement on salvation, and it is for that reason that we declare the pope wrong! Totally wrong! Tragically wrong! Truthless and wrong! How sad that so many precious people trapped in Catholicism are fed something so confusing and so totally wrong about a matter so eternally vital as the subject of salvation!

Let us be clear: Salvation is not a subject on which the Catholic Church has a monopoly (as the September 5 document asserted). In fact, since they do not teach salvation as the Bible teaches it, we are unhesitant to say that their message is totally off the mark.

Furthermore, salvation cannot be attained (as the pope's December 6 statement declares) by living the precepts of the Sermon on the Mount. As wonderful as the teachings of Jesus are on the Christian life, "living the life" does not secure salvation for sinners! We further reject outright the papal claim that those who live an exemplary life will be saved even if they do not believe in Jesus! This is unscriptural; in fact, it is against the Scripture!

False Gospels Pervert the True Message

"I marvel that ye are so soon removed from him that called you into the grace of Christ unto another gospel:

"Which is not another; but there be some that trouble you, and would pervert the gospel of Christ.

"But though we, or an angel from heaven, preach any other gospel unto you than that which we have preached unto you, let him be accursed.

"As we said before, so say I now again, If any man preach any other gospel unto you than that ye have received, let him be accursed."— Gal. 1:6–9.

Folks, please hear the Scripture on this! Salvation is a subject of such eternal magnitude that if we allow these false prophets to give out their false propaganda and let it go unchallenged, then we are as guilty as they are!

Lutherans Admit They Too Are Deficient

In the December 18, 2000, issue of *Christian News,* a Lutheran newspaper, the editor acknowledges that they too do not have a clear message going forth on salvation.

A survey taken by Lutheran Brotherhood shows that the majority of Lutherans similarly believe that as long as a person does good, even if he does not believe in Christ, he will get to Heaven.

Most of the major denominations today, including the Roman Catholic Church and the Evangelical Lutheran Church in America, either teach or allow their theologians to teach that Jesus Christ is not the only way to Heaven and that Christianity is not the only true and saving faith.

—CHRISTIAN NEWS, 12/18/00

So somehow the average Lutheran churchgoer believes he can work his way to Heaven. Apparently millions of them go to church without ever being told the real story, the truth of God about salvation.

Ecumenical Movement Minimizes Salvation Truth

While giving lip service to the subject, many of the ecumenical groups have so defined *salvation* that when they use the word, it doesn't mean the same thing as what the Bible says. Human opinion, denominational preference, political correctness and a host of other unsteady influences have been given legitimacy; and the Bible has been shuttled to the lower shelf without respect.

When these ecumenical gatherings occur, there is no standard on what salvation is; therefore, even the speakers may believe a wide variety of things on this most basic matter. It's no wonder the average man on the street is so confused!

Some Baptists Are Just as Bad!

Just as we speak candidly about the false message of Catholics, Lutherans and others, in like manner we give no place of comfort to some who wear the Baptist name but who, like these others, have misrepresented the Lord on salvation! When Baptist folks try to add to the equation so that salvation is made difficult or so that certain "evidences" of life are made essential to salvation, then they too are wrong!

Any such tinkering with the message of salvation is just as bad when a Baptist does it as when a Catholic or Lutheran does it.

(1) Some Baptists confuse salvation and sanctification. Salvation is by grace through faith—total: nothing more, nothing less! When you insist that a person exhibit a certain level of spiritual maturity before agreeing that he's saved, you've missed the mark and messed up the message of salvation!

First, there is salvation. Then comes sanctification. It is always in that order! Salvation is instantaneous, while sanctification is progressive. Some get saved and mature very slowly. Their slow progress should never be a basis of judgment to cast doubt on their salvation. Others struggle for years to get their lives straightened out and fail often in the process, but it doesn't mean they're not saved! The very fact they have a struggle may be in fact evidence that they are truly saved. A born-again heart is uncomfortable with ongoing carnality in the life; thus the struggle. But so often the lack of progress is wielded as a weapon of criticism—and that in itself may reflect a distorted view of the Bible doctrine of salvation!

(2) Some Baptists press repentance too hard! By that I mean they make repentance the main ingredient of salvation. Again, in so doing, lifestyle is made the main thing, and salvation's true Bible message is askew.

"But isn't repentance vital to salvation?" someone will surely want to know. Indeed! And I believe the one really definitive passage on that is Acts 20:21:

"Testifying both to the Jews, and also to the Greeks, repentance toward God, and faith toward our Lord Jesus Christ."

"Repentance" means "a change of mind," and Acts 20:21 states it is directed toward God—that is, it is a "change of mind" about God.

When men are made to focus on their sin primarily, they may have regrets or they may have sorrow, but rarely do they have a "change of mind." But when they have a "change of mind" (repent) about God, they will automatically see themselves for the awful, wicked sinners they are and thus "change their mind" (repent) about their wicked ways. Men do not typically understand their unholy ways until first they have seen the holiness of God (see illustration of this in Isaiah 6:1–5).

But be sure you stick with the Scripture on this! Bring people to God, and then they will deal with their sin! Too often some of our folks bring them to their sin first and then try to get them to God. The other way (God first, then deal with sin) is the biblical way.

(3) Heartless decision is also wrong. When people mouth words—even the right words—with no heart in it, it is not going to produce salvation.

"That if thou shalt confess with thy mouth the Lord Jesus, and shalt believe in thine heart that God hath raised him from the dead, thou shalt be saved.

"For with the heart man believeth unto righteousness; and with the mouth confession is made unto salvation."—Rom. 10:9,10.

A decision must be made, but it must be a decision of the heart. Mere form or intellectual assent is not enough! Note carefully it is a matter of "the heart" and "the mouth." Heartless expressions are empty and without substance. When you go after sinners, don't be content with halfhearted approval; go for the heart. Otherwise, you have failed, and miserably so!

So we urge upon our Baptist brethren, who have by and large been faithful with the message of salvation, to let no one pressure them into distorting the simple truth.

Bible Salvation Is the Only Real Salvation!

Let the truth be heard!

"For the Son of man is come to seek and to save that which was lost."—Luke 19:10.

"The Lord is not slack concerning his promise, as some men count slackness; but is longsuffering to us-ward, not willing that any should perish, but that all should come to repentance."—II Pet. 3:9.

The Lord Jesus Christ is the Saviour; and when He came to this earth, He came on purpose to fulfill a grand plan. He came to make

70

possible the salvation of sinners. Amen!

We must not let the garble of Catholics, Baptists or anyone else distort the great Bible message that Jesus saves all who by faith come to Him for salvation!

All of Us Must Understand We Are Condemned Sinners

"As it is written, There is none righteous, no, not one."—Rom. 3:10.

"For all have sinned, and come short of the glory of God."—Rom. 3:23.

Because we are sinners, we stand vulnerable before eternity. Sinners without a Saviour miss Heaven and go to Hell.

"For the wages of sin is death; but the gift of God is eternal life through Jesus Christ our Lord."—Rom. 6:23.

The Bible alerts us to two kinds of deaths, one where the body dies and the other called "spiritual death." In a word, spiritual death ultimately means going to Hell.

"For God sent not his Son into the world to condemn the world; but that the world through him might be saved.

"He that believeth on him is not condemned: but he that believeth not is condemned already, because he hath not believed in the name of the only begotten Son of God."—John 3:17,18.

There Is a Saviour, Jesus Christ

As condemned sinners, we cannot help ourselves; but God in Heaven made arrangements for us by providing a salvation—giving a Saviour to us.

"But God commendeth his love toward us, in that, while we were yet sinners, Christ died for us."—Rom. 5:8.

"For even hereunto were ye called: because Christ also suffered for us, leaving us an example, that ye should follow his steps."—I Pet. 2:21.

"So Christ was once offered to bear the sins of many."—Heb. 9:28.

Jesus Purchased Salvation for Us

"For I delivered unto you first of all that which I also received, how that Christ died for our sins according to the scriptures;

"And that he was buried, and that he rose again the third day according to the scriptures."—I Cor. 15:3, 4.

"By the which will we are sanctified through the offering of the body of Jesus Christ once for all.

"And every priest standeth daily ministering and offering oftentimes the same sacrifices, which can never take away sins:

"But this man, after he had offered one sacrifice for sins for ever, sat down on the right hand of God."—Heb. 10:10–12.

The death, burial and resurrection of Christ were the price of our salvation, and He paid for us exactly what was owed! Now we can come to Christ to receive the salvation we need!

Salvation Is Received by Faith

"But as many as received him, to them gave he power to become the sons of God, even to them that believe on his name."—John 1:12.

"For by grace are ye saved through faith."—Eph. 2:8.

"That if thou shalt confess with thy mouth the Lord Jesus, and shalt believe in thine heart that God hath raised him from the dead, thou shalt be saved.

"For with the heart man believeth unto righteousness; and with the mouth confession is made unto salvation."

"For whosoever shall call upon the name of the Lord shall be saved."— Rom. 10:9, 10, 13.

Having trusted Christ, we can be sure we are genuinely and truly saved.

"For God so loved the world, that he gave his only begotten Son, that whosoever believeth in him should not perish, but have everlasting life."—John 3:16.

"These things have I written unto you that believe on the name of the Son

*of God; that ye may know that ye have eternal life, and that ye may believe
on the name of the Son of God."*—I John 5:13.

Now, lest someone think I'm mad at the whole world, let me clarify what I'm saying. If and when anybody (Catholic, Lutheran, Baptist, whoever) anywhere (whether he or she be pope, preacher, student, whatever) tinkers with the doctrine of salvation, it is a great and grievous error, and it should not be allowed to happen without a voice of objection raised!

Bible-Believing Churches Can Be Trusted

The "Bible-believing" label may seem too broad a stroke as to be actually specific and helpful; but if it means that the church takes the Bible first and foremost as the fully trustworthy, totally reliable source of information and instruction and adds no human thought or tradition, then it means something significant!

If, on the other hand, it is a little Bible mixed with a lot of other things—such as tradition, preference, emotion, psychology, social agenda, etc.—then we think the red flag of warning should be at the top of the pole and the trumpet of alarm should be sounded with militance!

Salvation is by faith in Christ and not faith in any church! That is not to suggest the church is not important! It is, after all, God's idea (Matt. 16:18; Eph. 3:20, 21); and we should be very sure we are in a straight-talking, solid, scriptural church. If you are not in a church that is scripturally straight and scripturally strong on the great subject of salvation, you should without fail and without the slightest twinge of guilt get relocated.

Confusion on Salvation, a Deadly, Devastating Dilemma

Dear friend, you cannot trifle with something so important as salvation! And you should not tarry where God's great plan of salvation is tampered with.

Salvation is so important we must give full attention to getting it right. To miss out on salvation is a deadly, devastating dilemma!

Confusion must be settled based on God's holy Word, the Bible! My opinion, your preference and our conclusions do not make the grade! Despite the Devil's clever ploys to befuddle all of us totally, let me challenge you to give your fullest heed to the Bible!

For preachers, Sunday school teachers and others who profess to be Christians, when you talk about salvation, do your diligence to get the message communicated fully and without fouling it up.

Let's give ourselves to being good and faithful ambassadors of the great Saviour

"...who is the faithful witness, and the first begotten of the dead, and the prince of the kings of the earth. Unto him that loved us, and washed us from our sins in his own blood,

"And hath made us kings and priests unto God and his Father; to him be glory and dominion for ever and ever. Amen."—Rev. 1:5,6.

Scripture Index

Scripture Index

Scripture Index

77

Books Now Available
by
Dr. Shelton Smith

Books

Do It Again, Lord

Great Preaching on Revival

Great Preaching on Christ

Islam: A Raging Storm

SBC Conservative "Take-Over" Not a "Make-Over"

Pamphlets

Assurance Here and Now
(English and Spanish)

Al K. Hall: America's Most Famous Terrorist

Bringing Others to Jesus

Capital Punishment Revisited

Dear Mr. President...
What Christians Want Their President to Know

Fundamentalism in Focus

Hell Is for Real
(English and Spanish)

It's Easter and I'm Excited!

Liberal Choices;
Losing Causes

Living by Principle

Real Story of Christmas, The

This Same Jesus

When Unjust Critics Attack

Why I Still Believe the Bible

Order from your bookseller or from
**Sword of the Lord Publishers • Murfreesboro, Tennessee 37133
(800) 251-4100 • www.swordofthelord.com**

• Over 100 sermons each year • Tips on soul winning • Getting converts down the aisle • Bible studies • Answers to Bible questions • Columns of interest for every member of the family • Noteworthy news notes valuable to Christians

Order the SWORD OF THE LORD Newspaper
(800) 24-SWORD
or by logging on to www.swordofthelord.com